Pricing for Profit

Pricing for Profit

Curtis W. Symonds

AMERICAN MANAGEMENT ASSOCIATIONS

Library of Congress Cataloging in Publication Data

Symonds, Curtis W.
    Pricing for profit.

    Includes index.
    1. Price policy. 2. Profit. I. Title.
HF5416.5.S96   1982   658.8'16   82-71311
ISBN 0-8144-5748-7

First Printing

Everything is worth what its purchaser will pay for it.

Pubilius Syrus
Circa 42 B.C.

Contents

1

Pricing Objectives

Pricing is one of the most critical areas of business management. It represents the final judgment of value of everything that has preceded it, the final assessment of what all the time, cost, and investment required to bring a product or a service to the marketplace is worth. It is deserving of the most careful measurement, the greatest use of all available intelligence, and the most deliberate of judgments in balancing the required profitability against that allowed by competitive pressures. In concept, it calls for the best of management talent and management expertise. In practice, it usually receives far less.

Many companies will go to considerable lengths in developing truly sophisticated systems of accounting and financial reporting. This then becomes the foundation upon which an imposing structure of computer technology is built to provide an almost instant recall of accumulated costs and inventory balances, accounts receivable, aging, and the status of customer orders. The result is almost literally one of fingertip control of the flow of information in a complex combination of amounts, ratios, trends, and balances. Compared with the bookkeeping routines provided by handwritten ledgers at the turn of the century, the modern concept of a financial information system is as far removed from the past as the computer itself is from the days of the bookkeeper perched on a high stool laboriously casting up the accounts with pen and ink. The wonder of such progress, however, lies not so much in its achievement as in the fact that it is so poorly used at the very point where it is needed the most. All the time, money, and effort that has gone into creating the system is seemingly cast aside at the final payoff, the end product of the information system itself—its use in the pricing decision.

Pricing should be based on the expectation of reward, a reward for the time, cost, and investment both incurred and anticipated in bringing the product or service to the marketplace. It should be directed toward a measured amount, a computed requirement, based on recovering all costs, including the cost of capital employed. Specifically, it should be directed toward a price that will recover the costs of materials, labor, and operating overhead plus yield the rate of return required on the physical assets and working capital necessary for production and distribution. It should, in short, be the product of a disciplined approach, targeted for a specific objective based on a profit requirement. It should not start, as is so often the case, with an assumption of limitations imposed by competitive pricing or with a rule-of-thumb markup designed to recover recorded production, sales, and administrative costs and to leave a margin for profit on each dollar of sales.

Typical Approaches to Pricing

The first approach—that of simply following competition—assumes that someone else has done all the calculations necessary and that these calculations are basically correct and the competitive price the best that can be obtained. These assumptions are usually wrong on two counts. The competition has not made all the calculations necessary, such as including a cost of capital in the price arrived at, nor is the price the best the market will accept for possibly superior quality, better service, or greater availability. Such a course is not an example of a pricing decision; it is, in reality, an example of simply deciding not to make a decision, to avoid the time and trouble required to make an independent judgment. It is not management, but an abdication of management, not a considered measurement of objectives and requirements, but a simple exercise in acquiescence. It is basically the sign of a weak management that does not know how to go about pricing and mistakenly assumes that the other fellow does. Since the competition is usually following an identical path, the result is a case of the blind leading the blind, which can lead an entire industry into a swamp.

The second approach—the use of a markup over cost—starts off in the direction of measurement but usually falls far short of the need because of the inadequacy of cost measurement and cost definition.

The inadequacy of cost measurement will usually stem from archaic methods of product cost determination under systems of absorption costing. Such systems are based on a concept of "belonging" rather than cost behavior, and involve the allocation or sharing of common supporting costs among all products produced. This, of course, leaves the reported unit cost of any one product completely interdependent with the cost of every other product, since they are all subject to continual shifting as number of products produced varies, as the mix changes, and as levels of volume fluctuate. No independent appraisal is possible, but the manager concerned with pricing is aware that a large share of the reported unit cost of production results from arbitrarily allocated fixed overhead.

Reasoning, quite correctly, that this layer of cost is not directly related to the cost of production, the manager frequently uses such knowledge as justification for *marginal pricing*—that is, setting a selling price either below or just above the reported unit cost. In so doing, the manager sees the added sales volume he believes will be attracted by the marginal price as a means of recovering overhead—a philosophy that appears to be fully supported by cost accounting systems that develop an overabsorption of fixed overhead as *volume variance,* an apparent increment of profit going directly to the bottom line. What is not understood is that this bookkeeping fiction represents no more than an overstatement of costs charged to inventory and in fact encourages the use of marginal pricing. If repeated often enough, this type of pricing will indeed attract additional volume, often enough volume to require sizable additions in supporting overhead—a process that rapidly creates a downward spiral of profitability.

While the inadequacy of cost measurement can be damaging by itself, when it is coupled with an inadequacy in cost definition, the results can be disastrous. Defining cost is usually limited to a definition of the recorded costs of operations, limited by the accounting process to three basic elements of cost—the cost of materials, the cost of labor, and the supporting costs of such items as heat, light, rent, salaries, insurance, depreciation, taxes, and operating supplies, usually grouped into a category called overhead. This accounting approach reports the difference between income and these three elements of cost as profit, and in so doing, it leaves out the fourth element of cost—the cost of capital employed.

Although often referred to as an *imputed cost,* which carries a connotation of something less than real, the cost of capital is just as real as the cost of materials, and it must be met just as surely as the payroll, the rent, insurance payments, and taxes. The fact that it is not fully accounted for seems to support the idea of an imputed *theoretical* cost. That lack of accountability is not an indication of some sort of borderline type of measurement, but is, instead, a striking example of a measurement being used in the wrong place at the wrong time and for the wrong purpose.

Definition of Profit

The accounting measurement of profit evolved during the nineteenth century to meet the need of the day—essentially the need of the proprietor as the sole owner of the business. And since the owner and the supplier of equity capital were usually one and the same, measuring profit as a *remainder value* on the bottom line met the basic needs of measurement and the evaluation of results. The bottom line belonged to the proprietor, and acting as both judge and jury, he could decide whether the bottom-line profit was adequate in terms of his effort, his investment, and the risk of the enterprise. If on occasion he found it necessary to borrow money to help finance his business, the interest charges for borrowed funds were also accounted for as an operating expense, thus avoiding any need to deal with profit as a cost of capital. This measurement of profit worked well for the sole proprietor, but it became so ingrained as an accepted method of reporting that it carried over to a different type of business where it did not work at all well.

When the proprietary concept of profit was applied to the measurement of corporate results, several substantial differences in the structure of the two types of business organizations were completely ignored. The corporation is an entity unto itself and needs to be measured as such. The suppliers of capital are usually not the managers of the business, and the managers are frequently not the owners. Each group has a separate and distinct identity, and the compensation for each must be measured separately. Management is compensated in salaries and incentive awards; suppliers of debt capital have its use paid for in the form of interest; and suppliers of equity capital are paid from the remaining accounted form of profit found on the bottom line. Nowhere is the measurement of results presented for the corporation as an entity, leaving present-day profit reporting as a hybrid form of measurement at best. Part of the cost of capital—the interest cost of debt capital—has been accounted for. The greater part is missing—the cost of the equity capital itself.

In his article "Accounting for the Cost of Equity," * Robert Anthony points out quite logically that "equity capital has a cost, undeniably, although accountants do not record it; business would be far better off if they did." And since the cost of equity can be defined as the rate of return that the equity investor would find commensurate with the risk, it will be seen that the risk of the equity is, among other things, a function of the leverage imposed by the debt capital, whose presence places a prior claim on the profits available from operations. All this means, quite simply, that *interest charges on debt capital are not an operating expense in any business but a distribution of profits.* The profits of the corporation must thus be measured *before* interest charges, and since it is necessary to deal with net after-tax earnings, the measurement will be found in adding the net after-tax cost of interest back to the accounted net profit, a reconstruction of total earnings to be measured against total capital employed.

Thus pricing that attempts to deal with interest as an operating expense, as part of the cost to be recovered, is wrong in one of two directions. Either it has omitted the larger cost of equity from the pricing base, or if it has also computed a required rate of return on capital in arriving at the price it has doubled up on the cost of debt. Interest-bearing debt will have been included in the measurement of total capital employed and thus in the investment base on which a rate of return—a cost-of-capital element—is required. It will also have been included, incorrectly, as an operating ex-

Harvard Business Review, November–December 1973.

pense in the cost base. One approach or the other must be used, not both at once. If the cost of capital is to be included in the cost base, it must include the cost of *total* capital employed—equity as well as debt. If, on the other hand, the cost of capital is to be recognized in a required rate of return, the measurement of earnings must be *before* the distribution of part of the earnings in the form of interest payments to the lender.

Cost of Capital Must Be Recovered

A profitable approach to pricing thus begins quite early in the management process, and is one that requires this basic understanding of the profit measurement. It must recognize profit as *a cost of doing business,* an amount to be measured as commensurate with the risk of the enterprise. The profit requirement will probably be seen more clearly in this risk/return relationship when the requirement is shown in the second of the two methods indicated above. When expressed as a required rate of return on total capital, it will be seen that the measurement of risk and the resulting rate of return are both relative to other investments at varying degrees of risk. The rate of return required by the investor is thus a composite rate on debt and equity combined, a rate that simultaneously becomes the *cost-of-capital rate for management.*

Not only is the cost-of-capital a real cost, just as real, for example, as the cost of materials, the cost of labor, or the cost of the various elements of overhead; it can also be measured with at least the same degree of accuracy as charges for depreciation, a cost element that was also at one time omitted from the accounted measurement. Since the ultimate source of capital is money itself, the cost of money or funds in the monetary system becomes a base or controlling point of measurement. Usually expressed as the prime interest rate, it sets in motion the rates required of various types of investments such as savings bank deposits, U.S. Treasury bills, and commercial paper. As the risk increases, so does the rate of return required, a principle amply demonstrated in the marketplace.

Over a period of years, this relationship has placed the cost-of-capital rate for the nonregulated free enterprise business at approximately one and two-thirds times the average prime rate. The spread is first supported by the logic of relative risk, but is then more specifically demonstrated in the measurement of price/earnings ratios, which, over time, reflect a general correlation between the cost of money and the cost of business capital. If, for example, the average prime rate were assumed to be 12 percent for the foreseeable future, the after-tax cost-of-capital rate would be placed at 20 percent for the average business. This requirement would then be presented in the financial reports in one of two ways. The first would be in the more traditional accounting form of the income statement. (See Table 1.)

Here it must be noted that interest payments that the accounting process has treated as an operating expense are in reality a *distribution of profits*. As such, they have been added back, on an after-tax basis, to reconstruct the measurement of total earnings on total capital.

In addition, the statement includes a measurement of the average total capital employed to produce the earnings, a measurement frequently omitted in an ac-

Table 1. Traditional Income Statement.

Sales	$1,000,000
Cost of Goods Sold	500,000
Gross Profit	500,000
Selling and Administrative Expense	400,000
Profit from Operations	100,000
Interest Expense	10,000
Pretax Book Profit	90,000
Income Tax Provision	45,000
Net Accounted Profit	45,000
Net Interest Cost	5,000
Total Net Earnings	$ 50,000
Capital Employed	$ 500,000
Return on Capital	10%

counting presentation of profit. The resulting 10 percent after-tax return on capital, however, must next be compared with the 20 percent required, the cost-of-capital rate. This approach has several weaknesses:

1. The comparison to the 20 percent rate of return required is not shown in the body of the statement, leaving it to the reader to make a mental evaluation of the adequacy of the results.
2. The shortfall in dollars of earnings required to produce a 20 percent return on capital is not shown.
3. The statement ends up with "black ink" on the bottom line, a presentation that appears to reaffirm the accounting concept of profit as a remainder value.
4. The cost of capital is not shown except by inference when the comparison is made to the rate of return required.
5. It offers no direct approach to a pricing formula

that will ensure that all costs, including the cost of capital, are recovered.

Table 2 shows a second method of presentation, one based on the same information. While changing nothing except the total impact of the measurement itself, it shows an entirely different picture. This presentation actually shows exactly the same results as the first, a shortfall of $50,000 in total net earnings being the same as a 10 percent return on $500,000 of capital versus 20 percent required. Beyond that, however, several basic differences in interpretation emerge:

1. The shortfall is shown in dollars, not left to a mental calculation or comparison.
2. The fact that an *accounted profit resulted in an economic loss* is demonstrated for the first time.
3. All costs are fully accounted for, including the cost of capital.
4. A direct approach to pricing is made available.

Table 2.

Sales	$1,000,000
Cost of Goods Sold	500,000
Gross Profit	500,000
Selling and Administrative Expenses	400,000
Pretax Operating Margin	100,000
Interest on Borrowed Capital	10,000
Pretax Accounted Profit	90,000
Income Tax Provision	45,000
Net Accounted Profit	45,000
Net Cost-of-Debt Capital	5,000
Total Net Earnings	50,000
Cost of Capital @ 20%	100,000
Economic Gain (Loss)	$ (50,000)

That approach will be found in an analysis that combines the features of both of the two methods of profit reporting. It starts with a statement of earnings required and carries this discipline through to a pricing need. Using the same financial information already shown in the previous examples and applying it to a simple one-product company assumed to be operating at optimum capacity, the pricing need can be developed as in Table 3.

The discipline referred to will be found in the repetition of the word *required* throughout the calculation. The example itself is, of course, an oversimplification that obviously leaves many points unanswered. It serves, however, as a beginning that identifies the basic concept of pricing for profit—that is, that *pricing must be based on an objective rate of return on average capital employed,* not merely on a return on sales, and not simply to recover operating overhead.

Table 3.

Capital Employed	$ 500,000
Return Required	20%
Total Net Earnings Required	100,000
Less Net Cost-of-Debt Capital	5,000
Net Accounted Profit Required	95,000
Income Tax Provision	95,000
Pretax Accounted Profit Required	190,000
Add-Interest on Borrowed Capital	10,000
Pretax Operating Margin Required	200,000
Selling and Administrative Expenses	400,000
Gross Profit Required	600,000
Cost of Goods Sold	500,000
Sales Dollars Required	1,100,000
Actual Sales Dollars	1,000,000
Price Increase Required	10%

Refining the Cost and Investment Elements

Once this point is firmly established, the process can then move on to a step-by-step refinement of the cost and investment elements. Since the price required is now seen as a function of the combined costs of operations and investment, it becomes obvious that any overstatement of either one will drive up the computed price, probably pushing it beyond the level the market will accept. Customers are not likely to pay willingly for recovering excess costs or for idle investment, and a price based on such a structure will be found unworkable. This means that a true zero base approach must be used in each step of the calculation, locking in only the absolute requirements of the various segments of cost and investment in building the pricing base.

This should start with a careful analysis of the need for the amount of capital employed, an amount previously described as the sum of all interest-bearing debt plus the value of the equity amounts. This method of determining capital, however, will not suffice for the purpose of managing its use or determining the amount required. A second method must be used, one that will arrive at the same answer but will measure capital according to its use instead of its source. This is done by the simple expedient of measuring capital in terms of *turnover,* or its relationship to the annual dollar volume of sales. Since the dollar volume of sales will not be known until the price itself is determined, the calculation at this point will involve the question of interdependent variables—price determining the sales volume and sales volume determining the turnover rates for capital investments on which the price will be based. A mathematical formula to solve such an equation is not necessary, however, since approximate results will serve equally well for the purpose at hand. A reasonable estimate or assumption of the sales volume will suffice for developing turnover rates, since the rates themselves will be measured only to the nearest tenth in evaluating the need for capital.

Using the values given in the previous example for illustration, a total of $500,000 in average capital employed was assumed for a company doing $1 million in annual sales volume. By dividing the dollars of sales by the dollars of average capital, a turnover rate of 2.0 is measured for the use of total capital related to sales. Since this may or may not be found representative of the need, a further breakdown of the total must be made, describing capital according to its use as the total of all assets minus the sum of the non-interest-bearing liabilities. This approach then lends itself to a summarization of the elements found on the balance sheet into six basic groups, each of which can be measured in terms of turnover rates and the rates themselves compared to norms or averages for the type of business in question. Assuming that the sales, cost, and investment examples already used were those of a business engaged in light manufacturing, the breakdown might appear as shown in Table 4.

The adequacy of the turnover rates for each of the six groups making up the total capital will, of course, depend on the type of business being measured. Average rates by industry are available from several sources, chief among which is *The Annual Statement Studies,* published by Robert Morris Associates in Philadelphia. The analysis as presented in that publication expresses the values as percentages, measurements that

Table 4.

	Average Balance	Turnover on $1 Million Sales
Cash	$ 25,000	40.0
Accounts Receivable	125,000	8.0
Inventory	167,000	6.0
Plant and Equipment	200,000	5.0
Other Assets	88,000	11.4
Total Assets	605,000	1.7
Non-Interest-Bearing Debt	(105,000)	(9.5)
Capital Employed	$ 500,000	2.0

can be shown as the reciprocals of the turnover rates. In fact, the conversion of the turnover rates to a percentage of sales may well serve as a useful step to check calculations. (See Table 5.)

On the basis of this analysis—and using the comparison to turnover rates applicable to the business in question—it can then be determined which of the elements of capital does not conform to expected levels. If the investment is greater than normal, the result will be an overpricing that is likely to prove to be noncom-

Table 5.

	Turnover Rate	=	% to Sales
Cash	40.0		.025
Accounts Receivable	8.0		.125
Inventory	6.0		.167
Plant and Equipment	5.0		.200
Other Assets	11.4		.088
Total Assets	1.7		.605
Non-Interest-Bearing Debt	(9.5)		(.105)
Capital Employed	2.0		.500

petitive. If the level is lower than normal and the lower level can be maintained, it will provide a competitive edge in pricing. But if the lower level is due not to astute management but to an undervaluation of the asset, the result will be an underpricing that will lead to unprofitable results. The danger signals may then be said to lie in too much real investment or in too little apparent value. Capital, and the assets supplied by it, must be valued at estimated replacement cost if the resulting price is going to provide profits sufficient to eventually accomplish such replacement.

Once the capital base has been examined and any excess or deficiency corrected for pricing purposes, attention must then turn to the operating costs and expenses. Here the period expenses, or so-called fixed costs, should be examined first, since they constitute a somewhat constant base dependent more on management decisions for the amount involved than on any relationship to the dollar volume produced and sold. These in turn should be broken down by category, grouping those least subject to change, such as depreciation, insurance, local taxes, rent, and others that are not readily subject to change in the immediate term. This will leave a group of expenses, possibly listed by departmental identification, that represent functions of the business described in terms of payroll and related benefits, utilities, travel, advertising, and similar accounts over which management has a greater measure of discretionary control. These must be challenged, not on a percentage-to-sales or percentage-to-total-cost relationship, but on the *basis of need*. If the need cannot be demonstrated, the cost should be eliminated, both from the standpoint of operating efficiency as well as to ensure a proper base for pricing.

Next will be an evaluation of the variable costs of production and sales, a group more highly visible in most companies and one where the relationship can properly be measured in terms of unit costs or in percentages of the sales dollar. The unit cost of production may already be under close control, particularly if a system of standard costing is being used in the variable costs of production. A review here would thus tend to focus more on the design of the product and its inherent cost than on the question of operating efficiency.

The variable costs of selling may be a different matter, however, since such items as discounts and allowances, freight and warranty provisions, and sales commissions are not readily measured in terms of standard cost allowances or in efficiency rates. This area may well prove to be the one subject to the least amount of cost control, one where much is frequently "given away" in the pursuit of volume. Hence one very basic requirement at this level is to start a measurement in the reporting system with *gross sales* and to identify the group of variable selling expenses leading from gross to net sales as *controllable expenses,* expenses that should not simply be submerged into a measurement starting with net sales alone. In the pricing process, this will require working from the profit requirement back up to the level of net sales required and then dividing by a percentage to cover the spread between net and gross sales.

When all the foregoing steps have been accomplished, a beginning will have been made toward the development of pricing for profit. But since the pricing need will exist not for a theoretical one-product company, but for a multiproduct situation, such steps are no more than a simple beginning. Pricing a product must be based, not on total corporate costs and investment, but on the cost and investment required at the product level, a step calling for further analysis of the pricing structure.

2

The Profit Center

The example presented thus far of a hypothetical company that manufactures and sells a single product has made it possible to develop the pricing approach from a base of total capital employed and, by inverting the total corporate financial statement, to work from the bottom up by layering in the total costs of the company to arrive at the price required. It suggests a simple two-dimensional structure where management is operating a single entity, using single categories of cost and investment to price a single product.

In such a simplified structure, the management of the single product is the management of the company, since they would be one and the same. The total of all operating costs and expenses together with the total of all capital employed would exist in support of the one product, and management could actually confine its control of the business to this two-dimensional plane. Nothing else would be required.

Unfortunately, this limited view of a business structure is frequently applied where it is totally inadequate. Few if any companies actually exist on a single product base, and few companies can thus afford the simplicity of pricing from a base of total cost and total capital. To be workable, the concept must be expanded to encompass not only multiproduct, but multidivisional companies. It must be capable of providing a base whereby a single product group within a single operating division can be priced by itself on a return-on-capital concept, but that is adjusted to measurements applicable solely to the level of product management. Failure to do this will not only obscure the differing needs for pricing caused by the differing requirements of supporting cost and investment for the several product groups involved but will also inevitably ensure that the pricing of all products will be incorrect as to need and thus inadequate as to profitability.

What is needed is to move the measurement from the level of the corporate entity to the level of the *profit center,* an entity that can be described as a semiautonomous operating unit within the corporate structure. As a "little business within the business," it must be capable of being measured on all the basic elements necessary for an evaluation of profitability. It must have both responsibility and accountability for sales, for the cost of operations, and for profit contribution and investment. It will have far less than total responsibility for any one of these elements, since its semiautonomous status will mean that policy decisions, the supply of capital, budgetary controls, and other top-level functions and responsibilities will still reside with corporate management.

To the extent, however, that such authority and responsibility is delegated to the profit center level its measurement of profitability must stand alone and be capable of evaluation in terms of a return-on-capital concept. The profit center must exist in actuality, not simply on paper as a pseudo-measurement or bookkeeping exercise that attempts to create a statement of profitability without responsibility or to imply some measurement of accountability where no authority exists. Such attempts might include, for example, an allocation of sales income to a manufacturing unit, a level of management that had neither authority nor responsibility for pricing the product, for advertising, or for direction of the sales force. Similar attempts to impose a profit type of measurement on support functions, such as engineering or data processing, are equally unproductive, since no direct link to any form of profit measurement will be found to exist. To be valid, the measurement of the profit center must be confined to those operations where income, cost, and investment exist only for the activity and thus can be said to stand alone, uncontaminated by allocations of common cost or common asset usage.

Types of Profit Centers

By far the largest and most autonomous of all profit centers of measurement is the wholly owned subsidiary company. Almost completely independent in many respects, it closely parallels the measurement applicable to the parent company, namely the return on average total capital employed. It may be measured either before or after provision for income taxes, depending perhaps on whether the subsidiary is a domestic or a foreign corporation. The method of profitability measurement used requires virtually no change, however, although its goal or required rate of return may well differ based on the circumstances involved.

Beyond that, the subsidiary company itself contains various levels of profit centers, levels that do require different approaches. Chief among these and next in order of autonomy is the operating division. Here there will be substantially less independence, with authority and accountability still clearly measurable but contained to a much greater degree. Operating decisions, for example, will be made only within the limitations of financial budgets approved by higher levels of management. Pricing itself may be controlled at the corporate level, with sales terms and conditions frequently set as a matter of policy across divisional lines.

In like fashion, the management of capital will be limited to the management of only certain specific assets supplied by the common capital. At the divisional level, these will normally include the land, buildings, and equipment assets located at the division as well as the inventory of raw materials, work in process, and finished production on hand. If the products are also sold to a separate identifiable group of customers, the investment in accounts receivable will also be measurable as a divisional asset managed. Not included at the division level will be the cash and miscellaneous assets, nor the accounts payable and accrued expenses, the management of which is usually centralized for better cash flow and control.

On the operating side, many companies elect to make an allocation of corporate overhead to each of the operating divisions, a distribution that will clear out the corporate accounts and assess each division a share of the common cost. The allocation may be based on the sales volume of the division, on the head count of employees, or variously on the asset dollars invested. When challenged as to logic, the allocation is usually defended on the grounds that the division must carry its share of the load and therefore should be made aware of the contribution required to recover it. The intent is correct, but the method is one that does not serve the purpose intended. As noted in the earlier discussion of the concept of direct costing, the allocations frequently do no more than contaminate the measurement, leading to a series of mistaken decisions in the management of the operation.

Next in order are a wide range of possible profit centers related to sales distribution. These usually cut across divisional or even product lines since they are concerned solely with the profitability of the distribution of the product rather than with its origin. The most frequently measured unit in this group is the sales branch or sales territory. Here the sales volume and resulting gross margin can be measured against sales salaries and commissions, travel and entertainment expenses, sales office expenses, and so forth to determine the exact profit contribution generated by the territory or branch. With inventory as a common asset base for all sales outlets, the only assets measurable to the activity may be the accounts receivable, vehicles, and a minor amount of office equipment. This will, however, provide a sufficient investment base for measuring the profitability of this method of distribution when the profit contribution is brought together with the assets managed and measured as a rate of return.

In addition, similar profit center measurements might be made for the method of distribution as between sales to dealers and sales directly to the consumer. This analysis will generally cut across branch or regional lines and concern itself with global sales via the two methods. Here the emphasis may be placed on the difference in sales costs, with discounts allowed to the dealer compared with salaries or commissions paid to the direct sales force. Operating results may also be compared to possibly differing rates of collection of accounts receivable, the only asset usually measurable at this level of operations.

Other types of profit centers aimed at measuring sales distribution may include a comparison of domestic versus export sales, of government sales versus commercial accounts, or even of the profitability of major customers. Each of these will constitute a valid profit center of measurement, each with its own self-contained costs, its own separate use of assets, and its own sales income and gross margin. This group does not, however, provide any useful measure as a base for pricing a product.

That base will be found only in the measurement of the product line or product group, perhaps the most fundamental of all the possible profit centers of measurement. Here, the definition of what constitutes a product group for purposes of profit measurement may well differ from the grouping of items in the sales catalog. For measurement and pricing purposes, a product group must be one that *has common asset usage and common overhead support,* qualifications that will often run counter to the end use or classification of the various product models or catalog types contained within the product group itself. This becomes a critical point of measurement, since the pricing requirements of each of the several product groups will ultimately depend on the levels of support cost and investment needed to produce and market the item. And since no two groups can be expected to have identical support requirements, it is essential that they be grouped according to need rather than part number. As the only one of the profit centers that lends itself to a pricing approach, the product group becomes the focal point for profit planning. As such, it also requires a specific method for profit measurement. To accomplish this, the traditional two-dimensional view of business must give way to a different approach.

A Three-Dimensional Look

In effect, a third dimension lies in the fact that management cannot manage the total entity without first managing the profit centers that make up the total company. For the product group, one of the primary tasks of management is, of course, pricing. This task requires several changes in the method of measurement, changes that must start with a redefinition of terms. Traditional accounting must be replaced by what is often called management accounting, and traditional financial presentations must yield to a new approach to profit measurement, one that can evaluate the profitability of the product group entirely on its own merits, a stand-alone measurement independent of other product groups and devoid of any allocation of common cost or common investment. It will, in short, take on the appearance suggested by the three-dimensional look at profitability shown in Figure 1. The figure shows that only certain direct measurements are to be extracted from the usual financial statement and that many nonessential steps are eliminated entirely as having no bearing on the measurement of results at the profit center level. Starting then at the top, the data for sales of the product group are lifted out of the total and carried over directly to the new statement. The unit volume of sales, the average price, and the resulting dollars of gross sales are usually readily identifiable in most accounting and data processing systems and

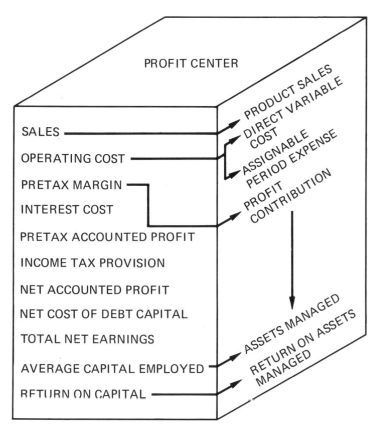

Figure 1. A three-dimensional look at profitability.

should present no problems in measurement. If discounts, returns, and allowances are involved, the same data are also generally measurable for the product group, permitting a continuation of the reporting down to the level of net sales.

What are not so readily identified are the segments of operating cost and expenses necessary for proper measurement of the profit center, segments that must be isolated from amounts that have no direct relationship to the profitability of the product group. First, the entire cost structure of the business must be analyzed and separated into the two basic categories of fixed and variable cost. In this process, only the direct variable costs of production and sales will be recognized as the cost of goods sold, and only those fixed or period expenses that can be classified as *assignable* will be charged to the profit center as a reduction of the gross margin earned in sales. This definition will exclude the allocation or sharing of common costs and expenses and will limit the measurement to those items that exist only in support of the production and sale of the product group.

The "stand alone" concept thus requires that if the product group were discontinued, the assignable period expenses would also disappear, with nothing left behind to fall back in another group or into a general category. Subtracting this group from the gross margin on sales will then leave a new measurement, not gross profit or accounted profit, but *profit contribution,* a clean measurement of profit center contribution to common overhead and corporate profit.

Next, in place of average capital employed by the total company, only those assets supplied by the capital and committed entirely to the production and sale of the product group will be measured. For a product group, these assets might normally include certain items of raw material plus the work in process and finished-goods inventories, equipment assets used only for the product group in question, and nothing else. There will be no allocated share of the land, buildings, or equipment shared by several product groups. Like the assignable period expenses, the assets managed must also be assignable, assignable in the sense that they would not be needed and would be completely liquidated if the product group itself were to be eliminated.

Finally, in bringing together the profit contribution and the average assets managed, the resulting measurement of the profit center will emerge as the pretax contribution rate of return on assets managed (ROAM). And as will be seen later, the pretax return on assets managed will be subordinate to, but fully integrated with, the total corporate measurement of the net after-tax return on total capital employed. To accomplish this will require a new approach to cost measurement, a revised definition of the unit cost of production, and a new understanding of the measurement of product profitability. In short, it will require a complete break with conventional cost accounting procedures.

Direct Costing

Traditional cost accounting is based on the full costing or *absorption costing* principle that all costs must be absorbed by the units of output. Dating back to turn-of-the-century usage, it is based primarily on the concept of "belonging"—that is, every cost must have a home, it must be assigned to a product or a service. This system worked well and would continue to work well for the company that had only one product in one model in one color. If such a company actually exists, a simple bookkeeping record would work equally well since all costs incurred would clearly "belong" to that one product and to nothing else.

The problem would come about when the company no longer had just one but had several products, products sharing the factory space, sharing some common equipment in production, and also sharing many common elements of supporting cost. If, for example, the company were producing three different products under these conditions, it would be necessary under absorption costing principles to share, or *allocate,* the occupancy cost of the factory space, the cost of indirect labor and supervision, and the charges for depreciation, supplies, maintenance, and so forth. Once these costs were fully allocated and new unit cost figures developed, the company might then add a fourth product that would require new assumptions, new allocations, and a major change in reported unit costs. In like fashion, it might decide to drop what appeared to be an unprofitable product only to find that many of the costs—allocated common costs—did not disappear with the product. The system, in short, served only to contaminate every cost measurement by making it totally interdependent with every other measurement. Today it has largely been abandoned by most well-managed companies in favor of a more logical approach.

That approach deals not with the concept of "belonging," but with a more basic characteristic, that of cost *behavior.* As shown in Figure 2, direct costing shows that in any business there are two groups of costs, each with its own behavior pattern.

The name "direct costing" derives from the fact that

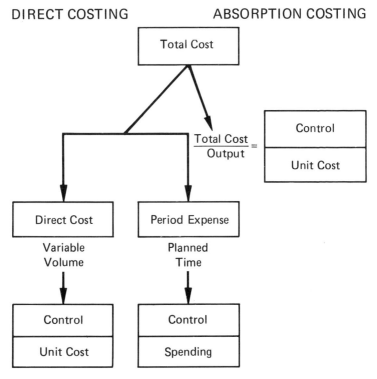

Figure 2. A comparison of direct costing and absorption costing.

primary emphasis is given to the segregation and measurement of those costs that vary in almost direct proportion to the dollar volume of production and sales. The method proposes that the *direct variable costs* in the factory be the only costs included in the unit cost of production, the only value charged to inventory, and subsequently the only elements appearing in the cost of goods sold. All other costs and expenses are identified as *period expenses,* because they are time oriented and independent of the short-term changes in volume.

Omitted from the calculation of unit costs, the period expense group is viewed as the cost of capacity, the cost of being able to produce whether capacity is fully utilized or not. Period expenses in production are thus expensed directly as incurred rather than being deferred through inventory to a later period when the goods are sold. This change not only recognized the different behavior pattern of the period expenses but succeeded as well in putting cost measurement into direct phase with cost performance. The basic behavior patterns of the two cost groups—one linear with volume and the other responding to volume change only in a series of increments over time—are illustrated in Figure 3.

The contrast between the direct and the absorption

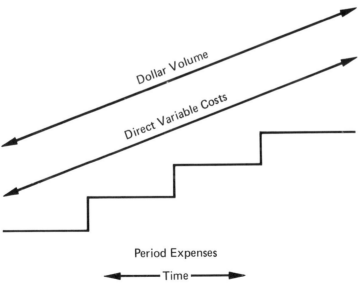

Period Expenses

◄────── Time ──────►

Figure 3. Cost behavior.

methods of cost measurement is best seen in a before-and-after example of a company reporting the profitability of its three product lines. Table 6 presents a typical statement prepared under absorption accounting principles. It shows a substantial loss for Product A for the year, while Products B and C recorded operating profits for the period. And since the net return on capital amounted to only a negligible 4.6 percent return for the period, management might well consider dropping what appeared to be a losing product in an attempt to improve the overall profitability of the business.

Taken at face value, this might be the only conclusion that could be drawn from the statement, assuming

Table 6.

	Product A	Product B	Product C	Total Company
Units Sold	50,000	30,000	20,000	100,000
Unit Price	$8.00	$15.00	$7.50	$10.00
Net Sales	$400,000	$450,000	$150,000	$1,000,000
Cost of Sales	330,000	270,000	100,000	700,000
Gross Profit	70,000	180,000	50,000	300,000
Percent to Sales	17.5%	40.0%	33.3%	30.0%
Selling Expense	60,000	67,500	22,500	150,000
Administrative Expense	47,000	39,000	14,000	100,000
Total	107,000	106,500	36,500	250,000
Pretax Profit	(37,000)	73,500	13,500	50,000
Income Taxes				25,000
Net Earnings				$ 25,000
Average Capital Employed				$ 540,000
Return on Capital				4.6%

that the costs of production were considered to be under control with normal operating efficiencies. If, however, the statement were to be redone on a direct costing basis, measuring contribution in place of accounted profit, a different picture might emerge that could lead to some different conclusions. To present the direct costing analysis, the following operating information would be needed, information that shows the manner in which various allocations of common cost were made in preparing the absorption costing presentation.

Cost of Sales

The manufacturing cost of goods sold has been determined as follows:

(a) Direct variable manufacturing cost per unit:

Product A	$3.60
Product B	6.00
Product C	2.00

(b) Period manufacturing expenses (fixed overhead) of $300,000 for the year are common to all products produced and were allocated to product cost on the basis of the number of units produced and sold.

Selling Expense

The total selling expense of $150,000 for the year was distributed to each of the three products on the basis of the net dollar volume of sales and includes the following general categories of expense:

General selling expense	$34,000
Advertising, Product A	20,000
Advertising, Product B	30,000
Advertising, Product C	66,000

Administrative Expense

The total of $100,000 in administrative expense was distributed to each of the three products as a percentage of the cost of sales.

This analysis would show that a total of $434,000 in common costs and expenses in the manufacturing, selling, and administrative functions were arbitrarily assigned or allocated to the various product measurements. These period expenses amounted to nearly one-half the total cost of operations for the year, but were deemed to "belong" to the product group measurement on a so-called full costing basis. The extent to which these allocated charges distorted the true measurement of product group operations can be seen when these arbitrary assessments are compared with the measured costs of production and sales for each product group:

	Product A	Product B	Product C	Total
Total costs reported	$437,000	$376,500	$136,500	$950,000
Measured costs	200,000	210,000	106,000	516,000
Allocated costs	$237,000	$166,500	$ 30,500	$434,000
Allocation % of totals	54%	44%	22%	45%

In actuality, these allocated costs had nothing to do with product cost or product profitability but were required in support of the business as a whole. Once this fact is recognized and the allocations simply eliminated, an entirely different picture of operating results will emerge. Table 7 shows a statement prepared on a direct costing basis.

In the new statement several important measurements appear for the first time. Chief among these is the measurement of gross margin on sales, stated as

Table 7.

	Product A	Product B	Product C	Total Company
Net Sales	$400,000	$450,000	$150,000	$1,000,000
Direct Cost of Sales	180,000	180,000	40,000	400,000
Gross Margin	220,000	270,000	110,000	600,000
P/V Ratio	55.0%	60.0%	73.3%	60.0%
Assignable Period Expense	20,000	30,000	66,000	116,000
Profit Contribution	200,000	240,000	44,000	484,000
Percent to Sales	50.0%	53.3%	29.3%	48.4%
Nonassignable Period Expenses				
Manufacturing				300,000
Selling				34,000
Administrative				100,000
Total Nonassignable				434,000
Pretax Profit				50,000
Income Tax Provision				25,000
Net Earnings				25,000
Average Capital Employed				540,000
Return on Invested Capital				4.6%

the "P/V ratio," or profit-to-volume ratio. Since the direct variable cost of goods sold represents constant unit costs, this means that the P/V ratio will be a constant percentage at any level of volume. It will change only with a change in the selling price or with a change in the direct variable cost of production; volume alone will not change the ratio. This measurement thus offers an important new tool in planning, budgeting, forecasting, and reporting. Above all, it becomes a vital part of the pricing formula. The contribution percentage to sales, on the other hand, will be a changing figure at every increment of volume, since its measurement is affected by the introduction of the assignable period expenses, a level of cost that itself will not change with short-term changes in volume.

Even with the statement of operations thus fully converted to direct costing, the report will remain incomplete and fall short of measuring profitability until the final element is added. The missing fourth element of cost, the cost of capital employed, must be represented in the profit center report in terms of the asset support required to produce the sales, to earn the gross margin, and to provide the profit contribution of the product group. Since the production facilities in the example shown were found to be an asset common to all three product groups, the assets managed would be limited to the following:

INVENTORIES

Product A	$ 60,000
Product B	100,000
Product C	40,000

ACCOUNTS RECEIVABLE

Product A	35,000
Product B	75,000
Product C	15,000

Combined, the two asset accounts represent the total asset investment attributable solely to each of the three product groups, assets that would not exist if the product groups themselves were to be eliminated. When this final step is added to the direct costing measurement of operations, a complete financial report of relative profitability by product group becomes available for the first time, a report that also demonstrates the complete integration of return on assets managed by product group with the absolute measurement of return on total capital employed for the company. (See Table 8.)

In this final statement, Product A, the product group showing an operating loss of $37,000 under absorption costing measurements, emerges as the most profitable of the three, with a 210 percent rate of return on assets managed. It did not have the highest gross margin percentage as measured by the P/V ratio, nor did it have the highest rate of profit contribution, falling in between the other two products on both counts. What it did have was by far the highest turnover rate for assets managed, a factor showing far less need for investment to produce the operating results.

One thing that has not changed in the new statement, however, is the low 4.6 percent net rate of return on total capital employed. The measurement of return on assets managed is simply a relative measurement of profitability, one showing the relative ranking of the three product groups. The absolute measure of total profitability is, of course, found only in the return on capital employed. The connection between the two measurements forms an important link in the chain of measurements leading up to the pricing need. It is demonstrated in the fact that the aggregate ROAM of 149 percent produced only 4.6 percent in the after-tax return on capital, an integration of the two measurements that leads to the final step in the development of the pricing formula. This can be done by simply in-

Table 8.

	Product A	Product B	Product C	Total Company
Net Sales	$400,000	$450,000	$150,000	$1,000,000
Direct Cost of Sales	180,000	180,000	40,000	400,000
Gross Margin	220,000	270,000	110,000	600,000
P/V Ratio	55.0%	60.0%	73.3%	60.0%
Assignable Period Expense	20,000	30,000	66,000	116,000
Profit Contribution	200,000	240,000	44,000	484,000
Percent to Sales	50.0%	53.3%	29.3%	48.4%
Assets Managed				
Inventory	60,000	100,000	40,000	200,000
Accounts Receivable	35,000	75,000	15,000	125,000
Total Assets	95,000	175,000	55,000	325,000
Turnover	4.2	2.6	2.7	3.1
Return on Assets Managed	210.0%	137.0%	80.0%	149.0%
Nonassignable Period Expenses				
Manufacturing				$ 300,000
Selling				34,000
Administrative				100,000
Total Nonassignable				434,000
Pretax Profit				50,000
Income Tax Provision				25,000
Net Earnings				$ 25,000
Average Capital Employed				$ 540,000
Return on Invested Capital				4.6%

Table 9.

	Actual	Required
Capital Employed	$540,000	$540,000
Return on Invested Capital	4.6%	20.0%
Net Earnings	25,000	108,000
Income Tax Provision	25,000	108,000
Pretax Profit	50,000	216,000
Nonassignable Period Expense	434,000	434,000
Profit Contribution	484,000	650,000
Assets Managed	325,000	325,000
Return on Assets Managed	149.0%	200.0%

verting the financial statement and by starting with the end result required, the objective rate of return on total capital employed. (See Table 9.)

In this process, a zero base approach is required in the step-by-step working back from the objective to determine the need at the profit center level. It is assumed in the example given, therefore, that no idle or excess capital is included in the base of $540,000 on which a net 20 percent return is required. It is also assumed that no unnecessary costs are built into the total of $434,000 in nonassignable period expenses. With this approach, it is seen that a 20 percent return on capital will require a return of 200 percent on the assets managed at the profit center level of measurement. The total need for the company in terms of profitability is thus translated into a specific requirement for the profit center, a requirement that will serve as a base for pricing at various levels of volume.

3

The Pricing Curve

It is undoubtedly well understood as a business axiom that price has a relationship to volume, that greater volume will in effect spread the overhead over more units of production, thus lowering the reported cost per unit and permitting a lower price. The logic of this statement may be clear, but the arithmetic unfortunately is not. The problem in the mathematics of measurement lies in the lack of visibility that the statement creates, where the idea of spreading the overhead fails to recognize that as the volume increases so eventually will the overhead. Since the volume and the required supporting costs will also rise at varying rates, one linear and the other incremental, no acceptable framework for pricing is provided.

The pursuit of the higher volume required to justify the lower prices can frequently lead to a downward spiral in profitability. In many cases, the added volume indicated will be so far in excess of capacity that major new investment and substantial increases in overhead costs will be required to produce it, factors that will obviously work against any justification for the lowering of prices in the first place.

What is needed is a framework that will provide a balance between price, cost, and investment, a framework that will work as a control in the pricing decision process. That framework must start with a plan for sales volume, expressed as an attainable share of market if such a measurement is available. This should be the starting point in any business, since the market itself will be the ultimate controlling factor in determining what volume should be produced at what price. The targeted volume or market share may then be planned in stages, based either on anticipated growth of the market itself or on estimates of the company's ability to capture the planned volume of sales. This planning will lead to the second step, the need to integrate market planning with capacity to produce.

Defining Capacity

Capacity can be measured for any business, but in order to be measured, it must first be defined. Maximum capacity—capacity to produce around the clock seven days a week—would be a useful base of measurement in very few companies. It is the base used in some mining operations where capital investment is so heavy that the economics of the situation dictate continuous use of the equipment. But for the average business engaged in manufacturing or merchandising, it would be far in excess of an economic capacity.

A more useful measurement would describe capacity in terms of *optimum availability,* a description that takes into account the limiting factors that determine the optimum balance for any business. The factors that limit capacity will, as noted, start with the marketplace as the ultimate control. It would make little sense to develop productive capacity in excess of marketability, since the excess capacity would prove both idle and nonrecoverable as to cost and investment. Productive capacity, in turn, may be dictated by floor space, by equipment, by the availability of raw material, or in many instances by the supply of labor. An average capacity for light manufacturing industries is frequently placed at a two-shift operation, five days a week. For merchandising businesses, the optimum capacity may be found in six-day operation on a single shift, for example. Although never precise or always constant, capacity exists and is susceptible to reasonable measurement.

Pricing Analysis at Various Levels of Capacity

The next step is to measure the planned *utilization* of capacity, since the optimum price will be found at the point of optimum usage. To test this approach, a pricing model will be developed for Product C, based on the information given in the preceding chapter. This product was the least profitable of the three, with an 80 percent return on assets managed as compared with the 200 percent rate required to meet the targeted 20 percent after-tax return on capital. In developing the pricing need for this product, the analysis must start with measurements of the cost and investment required at several different levels of volume or utilization of capacity. At least five levels of capacity are recommended for measurement in order to construct the pricing curve. For Product C, this might appear as shown in Table 10. These figures are based on the as-

Table 10. Pricing Analysis for Product C.

Utilization of Capacity	20%	40%	60%	80%	100%
Units of Production	10,000	20,000	30,000	40,000	50,000
Direct Cost per Unit	$2.00	$2.00	$2.00	$2.00	$2.00
Assets Managed Inventory	$30,000	$40,000	$47,500	$50,000	$52,500
Accounts Receivable	10,000	15,000	17,500	20,000	22,500
Total Assets	40,000	55,000	65,000	70,000	75,000
Return on Assets Required	200%	200%	200%	200%	200%
Profit Contribution Required	80,000	110,000	130,000	140,000	150,000
Assignable Period Expense	60,000	66,000	70,000	75,000	80,000
Gross Margin Required	140,000	176,000	200,000	215,000	230,000
Direct Variable Cost	20,000	40,000	60,000	80,000	100,000
Sales Required	160,000	216,000	260,000	295,000	330,000
Price/Direct Variable Cost Ratio	8.0	5.4	4.3	3.7	3.3
Breakeven Ratio	4.0	2.7	2.2	1.9	1.8

sumption that the present level of operations represents only a 40 percent utilization of rated capacity.

From this it can be seen that unit volume will change up or down in direct proportion to the change in the rate of capacity utilization. And while this relationship is linear, the unit cost of production will be found as a constant, a behavior pattern emanating from the fact that the direct variable cost dollars are themselves also linear with volume. With this as background, the first measurement can be made at 40 percent of capacity, the assumed present level of operations where known cost and investment figures are already available. (See the second column of Table 10.)

The measurement starts by literally inverting the typical financial statement and starting with the investment required, in this case the assets managed. Next, the 200 percent rate of return previously arrived at as a requirement is applied to the total assets to develop a measurement of the profit contribution *required,* a key word that will be repeated again and again throughout the analysis. The assignable period expense—expense that exists solely in support of the product—is then added to the profit contribution as a means of working back to the level of gross margin required. To this is added the direct variable cost of goods sold, arriving at the sales dollars required, a figure that, if attained at the cost and investment levels assumed in the calculation, would yield a 200 percent return on assets managed and in turn assure the 20 percent net return on capital for the company.

At 40% of capacity, if Product C were in fact a single product item, the sales dollars required, $216,000, could be divided by the 20,000 units produced at that level of capacity to yield a price of $10.80 a unit as the price required for full profitability. This, however, would restrict the usefulness of the measurement to a single product situation, a concept that would have limited value in any practical application. What is needed is a measurement or formula that can be used on any number of product types or catalog items contained within the product group itself. Since the product group involves *common asset usage and common overhead support,* it will be seen that individual products within the group, each having its own separate direct unit cost, can be priced by a single formula developed for the group as a whole. To do this, the sales dollars required are simply divided by the direct variable manufacturing cost of goods sold to arrive at a *price/direct variable cost ratio,* in this instance a ratio of 5.4 to 1.0 In other words, the unit direct cost of any individual product within the group would be multiplied by 5.4 to determine the required selling price.

One final step is needed in order to set a floor, or absolute minimum pricing level: the calculation of a breakeven multiplier or breakeven price/direct variable cost ratio. Since "breakeven" in this case will mean breakeven only at the profit contribution level—with nothing left to cover common cost or common investment—the measurement can be done very simply as follows:

Sales Dollars Required	$216,000
Less Contribution Required	110,000
Breakeven Sales	$106,000
Divided by Direct Cost	40,000
Equals Breakeven Ratio	2.7

The entire process is then repeated at another level of utilization, in this example at 20 percent of capacity. (See Table 10.)

The analysis of the cost and investment needs at

different levels of capacity should be based on the *need* for cost and the *need* for investment to support operations at the level of volume being measured. This would start with the need for inventory, $40,000 of which was found to be required in support of production and sales at 40 percent of capacity. At 20 percent of capacity, the output will be cut in half, but it is not likely that inventory levels can be reduced at the same rate. The level of the raw material portion of the inventory may be dictated by the economic order quantity and the work-in-process inventory determined by quantities required at each work station. Only the level of finished goods inventory may be found, in fact, to vary to any marked degree with a change in the volume of output. For this reason, inventory investment is placed at a need of $30,000 at 20 percent of capacity, a decrease of only 25 percent on a drop of 50 percent in unit volume.

The investment in accounts receivable must also be based on expected need and not simply assumed to be proportional to the change in volume. Several factors will impact this need, factors often working in opposite directions at the same time. First, the lower volume will of itself serve to reduce the balance in direct proportion to the output. Opposing this should then be the expectation of higher prices required at the lower utilization of capacity, a factor that will drive the level of investment back up. As a final factor—one that may move the balance in either direction—the question of sales terms, discounts, credit policies, and collection efforts must be considered. Bigger discounts offered in attempts to build volume back up will of course reduce the balances due from customers. Collection efforts, on the other hand, with volume at only 20 percent of capacity, may be more relaxed with the few accounts remaining, pushing the balances up again. All things considered, the assumed need in this example is placed at $10,000 for a net reduction of one-third on the 50 percent fall-off in volume.

In like fashion, the assignable period expense support must be challenged as to need. Here it is assumed that all the various elements of expense have been examined in detail, resulting in a step level of change to $60,000, or only a 10 percent reduction in going to a 20 percent level of capacity.

The final calculation of the direct variable cost required is the only step in the calculation that will be done as a direct ratio, a rate of change that will be directly proportional to the change in utilization itself. This is one of the virtues of the direct costing concept as discussed earlier and identifies the basic behavior pattern of variable cost.

Finally, estimates are prepared at the remaining three levels of volume, with investment and cost support requirements again based on expected need. (See last three columns of Table 10.) The logic that suggested asset accounts would not drop in proportion to volume on the down side applies here also, and only moderate increases are indicated on the up side. Assignable period expenses, displaying an expected time-oriented behavior pattern, have also increased only moderately and in incremental steps over the range of volume. The resulting price/direct variable cost ratios—ranging from a high of 8.0 to 1.0 at the low volume level to 3.3 to 1.0 at full capacity—suggest a wide range of prices required to meet the same profit objective (namely a constant 200 percent return on assets managed) *at any level of volume* within the limits of optimum capacity. The range in breakeven ratios also suggests a measurable set of limits on the down side, below which volume would be priced at an out-of-pocket loss.

Drawing the Pricing Curve

To be put into perspective, these ratios must be brought together in the form of a *pricing curve,* the end product of all the judgments and measurements that have gone into the detailed pricing analysis. The curve should be drawn as accurately as possible, since it will be used as the final pricing tool for the product group. To accomplish this, it is necessary to plot the price/direct variable cost ratios and also the five points of capacity utilization as accurately as possible. The use of graph paper scaled on an arithmetic grid is recommended, with the pricing ratios on the vertical axis and the utilization of capacity percentages on the horizontal axis. In connecting the several points plotted at the different levels of capacity, the use of a french curve will provide the natural shape of the curve indicating the pricing ratio required at any intermediate point of volume. Such a pricing curve based on all the assumptions and measurements used for Product C would thus appear as shown in Figure 4.

With completion of the pricing curve, the company has a measurement of the exact *need* for pricing at any level of capacity. If the company sets prices at any point on the top curve, it will get exactly the rate of return required, provided of course that all the assumptions that went into the development of the curve itself remain valid. It also has an exact measurement of prices at any level of capacity that will stop just short of an

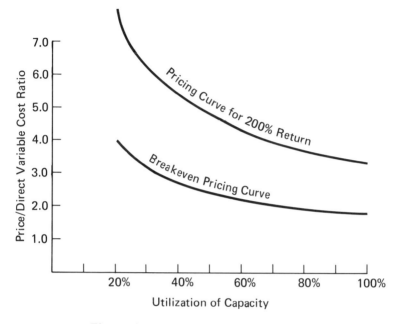

Figure 4. Pricing curve for Product C.

out-of-pocket loss. In short, it has a pricing road map of exactly where to go and where not to go in planning the relationship of price to volume. It will no longer have to deal with the vague belief that lower prices, higher volume, and spreading the overhead are all somehow working together for increased profitability. It now *knows* the exact impact of bringing volume, cost, and investment together with pricing with the assurance that all factors have been covered.

All factors, that is, except the final and perhaps most important one of all: What will the market allow? What will competitive prices be in comparison with the price *required* on the pricing curve? These all-important questions are left to the very end for a reason. Too often they are used as the starting point, as the only basis for setting a price in the first place. When this is done, the company has no real idea of the price it needs, just the price it believes it can get in competition. Only after the fact, when profits turn out to be less than adequate, does the pricing need become evident.

The need must come first if pricing decisions are to be made on a rational basis. It must come first if management is going to be aware of the consequences of following competition and in some cases of the need to drop a product or possibly to redesign it for lower cost *before* losses are incurred.

Competitive Pricing

Once the need has been shown by the pricing curve, the question of a competitive price can be handled quite readily. The company need only take the best competitive price and divide it by its own direct variable cost for the unit. The competitor's cost is of no great concern and probably is not available even as a rough estimate anyway. The competitor's price is all that is needed. By dividing it by its own direct variable unit cost of production, the company will then be able to add the competitive pricing to its own pricing curve.

If, for example, the competition were pricing at four times the unit cost for Product C, the competitive price would appear at 4.0 on the vertical axis. (See Competitive Price #1, Figure 5.) A horizontal line drawn from the price/direct variable cost ratio of 4.0 shows that such a price would intersect the breakeven curve at only 20 percent of capacity, an ideal situation. Extending the

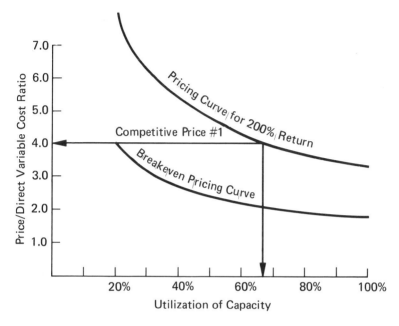

Figure 5. Product C pricing curve.

line until it intersects the top curve shows that the profit curve would be reached at exactly 67 percent of capacity, again an ideal, if perhaps somewhat unrealistic, situation. The measurement, however, is serving its purpose in answering two basic questions: What price is needed for profitability, and what will competition allow? In this example, the two answers coincide very nicely. In actual practice, they usually do not.

A more likely example would probably be where the competition is far less accommodating, one where the competitive price is not so attractive. Such a situation is shown in Figure 6 as Competitive Price #2, which has a ratio of 2.5 to 1.0 and offers breakeven results at 46 percent of capacity—not an unreasonable hurdle by it-

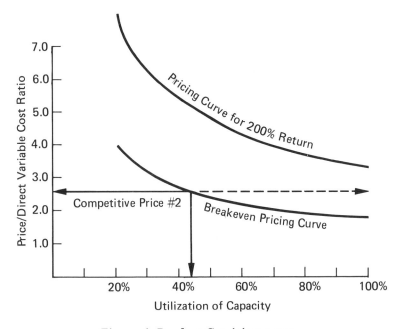

Figure 6. Product C pricing curve.

self. If the competitive price line were extended beyond the breakeven point, however, it would never intersect the profit curve, even at 100 percent utilization of capacity.

The consequences of following the competitive price in this instance are now clear. Based on the best judgments available, those that have gone into the construction of the pricing curve itself, the required goal can never be reached if the competitive price is used. There are now three choices available to management:

1. Drop the product group.
2. Follow competition anyway, since it will provide some contribution toward corporate overhead.
3. Rework the analysis used in constructing the

pricing curve to see what changes in cost and/or investment are required to make the competitive price acceptable—in effect, to bring the pricing curve down to intersect the horizontal line of the competitive price.

It is certainly the last of these choices that should be followed first, with the question of dropping the product held in abeyance as a last alternative. The second choice, that of simply following the competitive price to gain some measure of contribution, should be ruled out immediately as offering no more than a sure path to reduced profitability. Since the price available is judged to be below any reasonable level of need, it will normally attract increasing volume, volume that will eventually require added supporting cost and added investment, a combination that will ensure inadequate results.

The approach to reworking the analysis involves a series of steps. The first might be to determine the reduction in assets required to make the ratio of 2.5 acceptable at 100 percent of capacity. On the basis of the figures in Table 11, it might be decided that a maxi-

Table 11.

Ratio Required	2.5
Direct Variable Cost	$100,000
Sales Dollars Allowed	250,000
Gross Margin Allowed	150,000
Assignable Period Expense	80,000
Contribution Allowed	70,000
Return on Assets Required	200%
Total Assets Allowed	35,000
Total Assets Planned	75,000
Asset Reduction Required	$ 40,000
Percentage Reduction Required	53%

mum reduction of $5,000, not $40,000, is all that can reasonably be achieved at this level of operations. This change is then incorporated into the next step—that of testing the reduction required in assignable period expense to make the competitive price acceptable. Table 12 shows this to be $70,000, or an 87 percent reduction.

A reduction of this magnitude in the supporting assignable period expense would in all probability seriously jeopardize the sales volume and is likely to be ruled out as a viable solution. It might be assumed, however, that a reduction of $10,000 from the level of $80,000 planned would be an acceptable risk. If so, the lower level of expense would then be combined with the reduced level of asset investment, and the two incorporated in the third and final step—that of finding the reduction required in the direct variable cost of production, the only alternative left. Table 13 shows this to be $60,000, or a 60 percent reduction.

Unless the product has been overdesigned to start with, and operating efficiencies in production are considerably below any normal levels as well, there should be virtually no opportunity of reducing the variable cost of production by anything like the 60 percent re-

Table 12.

Assets Required	$ 70,000
Return on Assets Required	200%
Contribution Required	140,000
Gross Margin Allowed	150,000
Assignable Period Expense Allowed	10,000
Assignable Period Expense Planned	80,000
Period Expense Reduction Required	$ 70,000
Percentage Reduction Required	87%

Table 13.

Assets Required	$ 70,000
Return on Assets Required	200%
Contribution Required	140,000
Assignable Period Expense Required	70,000
Gross Margin Required	210,000
Sales Dollars Required	250,000
Direct Variable Cost Allowed	40,000
Direct Variable Cost Planned	100,000
Cost Reduction Required	$ 60,000
Percentage Reduction Required	60%

quired. At this point, every step has been tried, every possible reduction in cost and investment measured. The result shows that the competitive price cannot be made acceptable and that following it will continue to fall short of the goal required. There is now only one choice left—one that may prove difficult for managements unwilling to face up to the discipline the measurements call for. The product must be dropped from the line, because to continue with it at an inadequate price *would be to incur an economic loss even while showing black ink in the accounting sense of measurement.*

4

The Value-Added Concept

The pricing curve has been shown to be a precision instrument, one that will measure the exact pricing need based on all the judgments and estimates used in building the model. When the need is then compared to the price allowed in the marketplace, the difference is also shown as an exact amount, one that will further measure the precise impact in profitability when extended to an optimum use of capacity. Managements will benefit greatly from the use of these precise measurements. They must also learn when not to use them.

The step beyond the accurate use of the pricing curve is understanding that the mathematics of need must be tempered not only by the competition of the marketplace but by predictable patterns of price behavior inherent in the product or service offered for sale. These patterns are found in the concept of *value added,* a concept that refers to the basic conversion value from raw material to finished product. The degree of value added will thus have a direct correlation to the degree to which potential customers could create the finished product by themselves. A simple assembly operation, for example, adds very little value beyond convenience, since the assembly of parts is generally within the competence of the customer. The manufacture of a semiconductor device, on the other hand, is heavily dependent on high technology and investment, with a knowledge of solid-state physics beyond the reach of the average buyer. But while the wide range in value added between these two examples may be quite evident in concept, the impact of the differences on the pricing decision may be apparent only when specific measurements are applied. These measurements will, in turn, depend on the use of direct costing, a technique whose many benefits have already been described.

Breakeven Point Analysis

In addition to the simplicity of cost measurement and the visibility afforded for profit management, the direct costing system offers one further advantage. That advantage lies in the ready calculation of *breakeven point volume,* a calculation possible only with the complete separation of fixed and variable costs. The breakeven point is, of course, the point at which the gross margin from sales will equal the fixed costs or sum of the period expenses, leaving a zero balance in profit or loss. It cannot readily be determined under absorption accounting measurements, but can be calculated quickly under direct costing by means of the following equation:

$$\frac{\text{Total Period Expenses}}{\text{P/V Ratio}} = \text{Breakeven Point}$$

If this formula were applied, for example, to the figures previously shown on the direct costing statement for Product C, the breakeven point *at the profit contribution level* would appear as follows:

Assignable Period Expenses	$66,000
Divided by P/V Ratio	73.3%
Equals Breakeven Point	$90,000

The breakeven point volume of $90,000 could next be tested, or proved, by comparing it with the actual sales volume for the same period and then measuring the profit contribution of the volume difference above or below the breakeven point:

Actual Sales	$150,000
Breakeven Point	90,000
Volume over Breakeven	60,000
P/V Ratio	73.3%
Profit Contribution	$ 44,000

Measurement and control of the breakeven point is one of the more important financial tools of management. It is a measurement that is frequently neglected when business is good, when the current volume of sales is well ahead of the breakeven level of operations. And it is one whose presence becomes painfully apparent when business falls off. Breakeven points will inevitably increase over time as a business expands to meet a growing market, but short of actual sales growth, they will tend to rise on their own, developing an independent growth rate that must be controlled. Unless monitored on a regular basis, the increase in breakeven point may not readily be seen, nor its impact understood. Putting it into visual perspective, however, not only provides an increased awareness for management of its effects on profitability, but offers an added dimension as well, one pertaining to value added, which is available in the profile provided by the development of the breakeven point chart. Figure 7 shows such a chart for Product Group C.

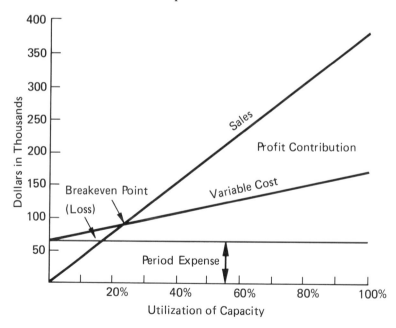

Figure 7. Product C breakeven point chart.

As in the pricing curve, the utilization of rated capacity is plotted at five different levels of volume on the horizontal axis. The vertical axis is then scaled in dollars measured in thousands, thus assuming a sales volume of $400,000 at a utilization of 100 percent of capacity. The assignable period expense total of $66,000 is then plotted as though it were a constant level throughout the entire range of volume. (It will not be constant, behaving in incremental steps from zero to 100 percent utilization of capacity, but an assumption of constant cost will serve the purpose at hand.) Next the sales curve is entered on the chart, running diagonally from zero capacity in the lower left-hand corner to the $400,000 level at full capacity in the upper right. The breakeven point, having been calculated at $90,000, is then measured on the vertical axis and plotted at that level on the sales curve. The final step is to draw the curve for variable costs. At zero capacity these will coincide with the $66,000 level for assignable period expenses, since with zero production and zero sales, no variable costs would be incurred. The variable cost line is then drawn to intersect the breakeven point, completing the structure of the breakeven point chart as shown in Figure 7.

The final picture shows a widening gap to the right of the breakeven point, with the spread measuring the increase in profit contribution as volume increases with a higher use of capacity. In like fashion, a loss or negative contribution is measured to the left of the breakeven point as volume falls off to zero. And since the chart is measuring breakeven point only in the sense of breakeven contribution, leaving nothing for the recovery of common period expenses or for contribution to corporate profit, the breakeven point will be found at a low percentage of capacity—in this example, at a utilization of about 25 percent of potential volume. When the same technique is applied to total company operations, rather than to a profit center, the breakeven point will normally be found at a much higher utilization of capacity, since all the period expenses of the business will have been included in the calculation. In either case, the breakeven point chart will present a picture of certain characteristics that will serve to identify the relative value-added nature of the product or service.

Volume-Sensitive Products

The breakeven chart for Product Group C also provides a measurement in another dimension, one that identifies the product as high value-added, showing that the product is volume sensitive in the marketplace. This means that the profitability of this product will be more responsive to changes in volume than to attempted changes in the price/cost relationship. A volume-sensitive product can be recognized by the following set of characteristics:

1. It will have a relatively high period expense level, high visually in the chart, and high as a percentage of sales.
2. It will have a low direct variable cost, one in the order of 30 percent to 50 percent of sales.
3. It will have a correspondingly high P/V ratio or gross margin rate, with the reciprocal of variable cost ranging from 50 percent to 70 percent of sales.

4. It will have a wide spread visually on the chart once the breakeven point is passed.
5. It will be a high value-added product or service.

The high value-added measurement is based on a high conversion value, one requiring the high technology and investment reflected in the need for a high level of period expense. The conversion value also reflects the fact that the cost of technology and know-how is equal to or greater than the basic production cost of material and labor, a factor that in turn commands a high gross margin in relation to variable cost.

Under these conditions, the management of profit becomes primarily the management of volume, since the price/cost relationship will be found to have minimal potential for profit improvement. If volume for Product C, for example, were to be increased from 30 percent of capacity to 50 percent, the pretax profit contribution, as measured on the breakeven chart, would more than quadruple, climbing from a little over $16,000 to more than $71,000 on a two-thirds increase in volume. By contrast, no comparable increase in profitability is potentially available from changes in the price/cost relationship for several rather obvious reasons. First, with a P/V ratio of 73.3 percent, the price is already high, with little room for upward movement between the 73.3 percent and a ceiling of 100 percent, a level beyond which variable cost would have to exist as a negative. Second, there is obviously not too much room for cost reduction in a product cost measuring only 26.7 percent of sales, nor is any appreciable amount likely to be pried loose from supporting period expenses—the expenses of know-how and technology required to produce the high value-added nature of the product in the first place.

The Demand Curve

Recognition of this fact places a limiting factor on the pricing curve, one that will show the probable reaction to price in the marketplace, a price-behavior curve that will override the plain mathematics of the price range indicated by the demands of cost and investment. This takes the form of a *demand curve,* one developed from an understanding of the market superimposed on the pricing curve itself. The demand curve for Product C might take the shape shown in Figure 8.

The demand curve shows, for example, that some volume—estimated at 10 percent of capacity—would continue to be sold at a price/cost multiple as high as 8 to 1. A basic demand for the product, in other words, would still exist even at an abnormally high price. The curve also indicates that any drop in price below the 4 to 1 ratio called for at 80 percent of capacity would not serve to attract more sales volume but would simply erode profits. Price, in other words, will not increase demand beyond a certain point.

Thus, the nature of the product—in this case, a high value-added one—puts price and cost considerations into clear perspective as having definite limitations at each extreme of the volume curve. At the low end, availability is of greater concern than price, since customers do not have the technology and know-how to produce the product for themselves. At the high end,

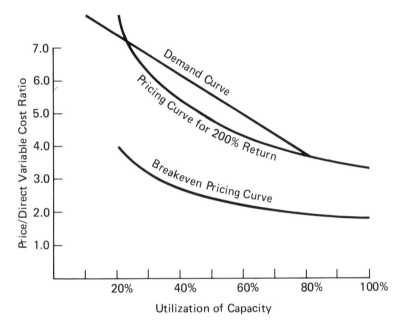

Figure 8. Product C pricing curve.

it becomes apparent that sales volume does not respond to price reductions, the demand being determined by need rather than by cost considerations. With
due attention to the price availability and to cost requirements and control, the basic thrust of profit management in the high value-added product is thus seen
as an *optimization of volume* rather than an extension of
the price/volume curve.

Price/Cost-Sensitive Products

In contrast to the volume-sensitive, high value-added
product, some products are at the opposite end of the

spectrum. They first of all have a low value-added content—that is, little if any value is added in the process of conversion from basic raw materials to finished product. This group would include assembly rather than basic manufacturing operations, and will be more representative of the distribution of goods than production. Low value-added also means that the customer can produce the product himself if necessary, that he is not dependent on investment or technology beyond his reach. Whether or not he chooses to do so will thus be determined almost entirely by price. The product is consequently identified as *price/cost sensitive,* an identification that leads to some opposite indications in the use of the pricing curve. It will have an entirely different appearance on the breakeven point chart as shown in Figure 9.

The price/cost-sensitive product has the following characteristics, measurements that also fall into a single if opposite type of pattern:

1. It will have a low level of period expense, low visually on the chart and low as a percent to sales.
2. It will have a high direct variable cost, on the order of 90 percent to sales.
3. It will have a correspondingly low P/V ratio or gross margin rate in the range of 10 percent of sales, the reciprocal of the variable cost.
4. It will have a very narrow spread on the chart once the breakeven point is passed.
5. It will have indications of low value added.

With this product, an increase in sales volume alone will do very little to increase profitability. The gap beyond the breakeven point opens very slowly, offering only modest gains in contribution for substantial in-

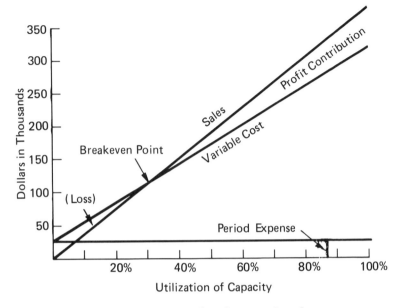

Figure 9. Product X breakeven point chart.

creases in volume. When the probable added cost of securing the higher volume is added to the picture, the probability of greater profitability through volume will be seen as severely limited. Attempts to reach a higher volume of sales on this product would normally call for increased expenditures for advertising and promotion, expenditures that would raise both the level of required period expenses and the breakeven point itself. In addition, if added discounts were also offered as an inducement for higher volume—a path frequently followed in promoting low value-added products—the margins would also be reduced, moving the breakeven point even closer to capacity.

If, on the other hand, prices were increased or costs were reduced or both, the gap would be widened and a measurable gain in contribution would follow. Unlike the high value-added product, where such opportunities were quite limited, this product offers substantial potential for improvement in both price and cost:

1. With margins at a level of only 10 percent of sales, an increase of just 1 percent in the selling price will yield a gain of nearly 10 percent in the P/V ratio.
2. Correspondingly, with direct variable costs in the range of 90 percent of sales, several opportunities for cost reduction should be available in a review of economic order quantities, in new sources of supply, or in a change in product mix.
3. Only in the level of period expenses will little opportunity for cost reduction be found. Inherently low in a low value-added type of business, this level of cost will not be susceptible to any major change.

The options for increased profitability on this product are thus clearly spelled out just as they are for a high value-added product—albeit in a different direction. The expected reaction of the marketplace to the price/cost behavior of the low value-added product can also be seen when a demand curve is added to the picture of the pricing curve for the product, as shown in Figure 10. In this case, the demand curve is clearly affected by price.

Here it is estimated that sales volume would approach zero at a price in excess of a multiple of four times direct variable cost and, conversely, that sales would continue to increase as prices were reduced. There is no fixed demand for the product at any price, nor is the need fulfilled at any given quantity. Since

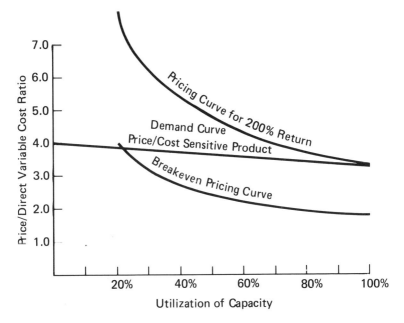

Figure 10. Product X pricing curve.

market demand will expand as prices are lowered, the optimum point on the pricing curve will quickly identify the crossover point between volume and profit.

Other Value-Added Considerations

Beyond the inherent value-added nature of the product itself, pricing decisions should give consideration to the value as perceived by the customer, a value that may bear little relation to the supplier's own calculation of worth. The perceived value may in some instances be found more in the somewhat intangible areas of reputation, quality, and service. In other cases, the product may represent a necessary but minor cost component of a customer's bill of materials, an item relegated to the 80 percent of parts that account for only 20 percent of the total cost, a classification that may put availability and reliability ahead of price considerations. In still other situations, prices may be less subject to resistance when the product offered for sale will be capitalized by the customer as a fixed asset to be depreciated over time. In many companies, the capital budget seems to be of less immediate concern than the operating budget, and a price that might be rejected if charged as an expense may be accepted without comment if charged as an asset on the balance sheet. The logic is obviously flawed, but the opportunity persists and should be recognized.

In summary, use of the pricing curve indicates many considerations and judgments that must be added to the pricing decision: competitive prices, value-added relationships, intangible factors—all must be taken into account before a price is established. In doing so, the pricing curve will be seen as a *measured point of departure,* a base from which judgments can be made with respect to the profitability of the final pricing action. Without it, the judgments are intuitive and without measurement or control.

5

Impact of Sales Terms on Pricing

The concept of pricing is frequently confined to the identification of the price per unit charged to the customer on the sales invoice, or as listed on the company's price sheet or in its catalog. The terms and conditions of sale, often shown in fine print on the back of the invoice, are not always seen as having any direct bearing on price. In reality, they have a substantial impact on the *actual price recovered,* and in many instances serve to completely negate the effect of the pricing decision. Some of the sales terms are readily measurable as to the effect on price; others are not, being either hidden from view or misleading as to interpretation. In total they constitute an integral part of the pricing process, and the effects of each must be measured on a step-by-step basis if the desired economic results are to be obtained.

Cash Discounts

One of the more obvious examples of pricing impact is in the measurement of cash discounts allowed for early payment. Typical is the discount of "2% 10 days net 30." First, the discount is a direct reduction of 2 percent in the selling price, a reduction that will usually be taken by the customer, even beyond the 10-day period allowed. Second, the offer of a 2 percent reduction for payment 20 days early—in 10 days rather than 30—amounts to an annual interest rate of 36 percent per year, a payment for the use of money far in excess of the bank rate for funds even in times of double-digit inflation.

Taken together, these two points add up to the fact that cash discounts seldom work as intended, that in practice they routinely become nothing more than a price concession. Management is not deliberately offering 36 percent per annum for the use of money, but an alert customer will make the calculation properly and be quick to take advantage of it. Furthermore, the fact that many accounts take the discount well after the time allowed is evidence that customers regard it more as a price concession than a reward for early payment. Some attempts are made by companies to charge back the unearned discount, a procedure that results in creating undesirable friction with their own customers, a situation the sales force would prefer to avoid.

Variations of the cash discount terms, such as "2%

10th prox," further complicate the picture by encouraging customers to bunch their orders around the first of the month to get the greatest leverage on the terms offered. This, obviously, can have the undesirable effect of creating peak work loads in order entry, shipping, and billing with consequent dry periods toward month end.

In short, cash discounts make little economic sense as payment for the use of funds and in practice become nothing more than a reduction of price. The great majority of companies have in recent years found it to be an awkward vehicle for price adjustment and have abandoned it in favor of net terms.

Net Terms

The *net terms* for payment of the sales invoice also have an impact on pricing, although for many managements an indirect and somewhat remote impact insofar as pricing decisions are concerned. If the price required is to be calculated on the basis of return on assets employed as shown in the construction of the pricing curve, the net terms will obviously create an asset called accounts receivable, a use of capital that must be recovered in the pricing process.

As previously noted, however, pricing based on the return-on-investment concept is used by only a small minority of companies, so that any connection between the tie-up of funds in amounts due from customers and the effective pricing is not even considered in most cases. And when the terms are then not enforced, with typical 30-day net terms stretching to an average collection period of 50, 60, or even 70 days, the "hidden discount"—the added cost not recovered in pricing—mounts rapidly.

If, for example, the net after-tax cost of capital is placed at 20 percent, as in Chapter 1, the equivalent pretax cost would be in the range of 37 percent for medium to large companies. Assuming that 30-day sales in accounts receivable have already been included in the pricing base, the cost of capital for a 30-day period will be recovered in the target price, providing the customer pays on time. If, however, the customer is 30 days late in paying—taking a net term of 60 days to pay instead of 30—the hidden discount will amount to a little over 3 percent at the annual cost rate of 37 percent. If payment is delayed another 30 days, the price concession will amount to 6 percent and so on.

This added cost of 3 percent a month for accounts receivable, moreover, is by no means offset or recovered by those few firms that charge (and collect) interest on past-due balances. The interest rate usually assessed seldom exceeds 18 percent per year, or 1.5 percent per month—a recovery of one-half the cost at best. This point is often lost in the process of measurement when profitability is confused with cash flow. If, for example, the company finds it cannot prudently invest idle funds at more than a 12–15 percent rate of return, it might view the annual 18 percent rate on past-due balances as a *substantial gain* in operating profits and be quite content to let the aging continue as long as the accounts were still considered collectible. This would indeed create both increased cash flow and increased accounted profit, *but at the expense of an economic loss.* Failure to earn the full rate of return required, again as noted in Chapter 1, must be recognized as a failure to recover all costs and hence as a loss in the economic sense of measurement.

The inadequate management of accounts receivable stems from two factors. The first has already been discussed—the failure to relate the cost of capital tied up to the net pricing effect, with the result further confused by objectives limited to accounted bottom-line profit and cash flow. The second factor has to do with motivation, or more correctly, with the lack of it. The collection of receivables is a management function that is all too often not performed by management. In many companies, it is a routine clerical task assigned to the credit and collection department, a function frequently reporting to sales management. Sales personnel are primarily interested in getting the order, not in collecting the money, and the level of importance given to the collection effort may well reflect this distaste for the function. The significance of asset management is again pushed to the background in many sales incentive or bonus plans designed for sales management. Many are based simply on total sales volume; a few are tied to gross margin or possibly profit contribution. Only a handful are usually linked to the collection of receivables, in effect to an incentive based on return on assets managed. When this final piece is added, two changes take place at once. The accounts are collected more quickly and the salesmen involved have taken a major step forward in understanding the basic functions of management.

Freight Terms

The only freight terms that have no pricing adjustment impact are terms of F.O.B. factory or shipping point. The customer pays the freight, period. Such terms are not only clean as to cost, but clean as to liability for loss or damage in transit, since title to the goods passes with delivery to the carrier.

But beyond this straightforward point of departure, there are several variations. Terms of F.O.B. destination are also clean *if the freight charge is included in the selling price.* Many times it is not, and the resulting cost becomes a significant reduction in the effective price. The company first adopts the freight to destination policy for Product A, a small component where the freight cost is a minor factor. It later expands into Product B, a heavy machined casting where freight is a major cost element—and then simply stays with its freight policy since "the customers are accustomed to it." A major hidden discount is now built into the system, and the reluctance to change policy may well carry over to a reluctance to price for its recovery.

Since F.O.B. destination also means that title remains with the shipper until the goods arrive at the customer's location, these terms have the further disadvantage of liability during transit. To overcome this latter objection, terms of F.O.B. shipping point, freight allowed to destination, are often substituted. This solves the question of liability during transit but leaves the cost impact with the shipper.

All the foregoing terms for freight discussed so far are generally well understood, and companies are aware of any cost involved, whether they feel the cost can be recovered in the price or not. The truly hidden cost seems to be reserved for the final set of freight terms, one that appears harmless on the surface. Terms that state "freight prepaid and charged" certainly suggest that the cost is fully recovered, prepaid for the convenience of the customer, and then passed through in total when added to the sales invoice.

One major supplier of steel castings followed this

policy, with freight bills in excess of $1 million a year being paid by the company and a subsequent rebilling and collection from its customers. It regarded the whole transaction as a "wash," acknowledging only the added clerical costs in accounting and billing required to keep track of the freight charges for each individual shipment. Over a period of time, the transaction was indeed a wash on the accounted statement of operations. Except for timing or occasional errors in billing, the freight charges and credits did cancel one another out. The company's attitude seemed justified—and yet a major reduction in effective price was taking place.

What the company overlooked was the fact that it was required by the Interstate Commerce Commission to pay its freight bills in 7 days. The company was then waiting an average of 67 days to recover these freight charges as part of its accounts receivable. Collections were chronically slow in its industry, and while the operating statement showed a virtually complete recovery of freight costs, the balance sheet reflected a net 60-day tie-up of funds at a zero rate of return. This was not reported as such in any monthly report to management, and no cost appeared as a charge against sales income. Nevertheless, a two-month tie-up of payments totaling $1 million a year could be calculated at a pretax cost of 37 percent a year for capital employed—a cost totaling over $1,000 a day for the 60-day delay in collection. The "wash" transaction was in fact a substantial discount in price.

Volume Discounts

Many managements are completely sales oriented, blandly assuming that profit will somehow take care of itself if the volume of goods sold can be pushed ever higher. To this end, a series of deals are made with large accounts, for lower prices in some cases, but more often for *volume discounts* and rebates. These should be distinguished from *quantity discounts*, a term generally applied to the price breaks calculated for increasing levels of order quantities. These, it can be assumed, have been determined on some rational basis and probably make good economic sense. The volume discount is quite different and usually makes very little economic sense, being a device aimed solely at a volume increase with no measured link to profitability.

The pricing curve demonstrates the price/volume relationship, showing how a lower net price can be justified with an increase in the total volume of sales, a total volume that then utilizes an optimum level of productive capacity. This can make economic sense, but a discount or rebate on the cumulative volume of selected customers will not add up to profitability, not if the total volume of all accounts is still short of the mark.

Granted that the device may at times be a necessary tool in the salesman's kit, it deserves better measurement. If, for example, the company sells its products at $100 per unit and then offers the customer a 10 percent volume discount for an order of ten units, the cost will be $100 in cash. The same offer made in terms of merchandise—one unit free with every ten purchased—could have the same appeal to the customer who is valuing the units at $100 each in his inventory. Just as valuable to the buyer but far less costly to the seller, the use of merchandise in place of cash can reduce the effective discount dramatically. With a P/V ratio of 60 percent, the seller would have a unit cost of only $40 in merchandise, and a 10 percent discount in the eyes of the buyer would cost only 4 percent on the books of the seller.

If giving a discount or price concession for higher volume can be said to make sense at one end of the spectrum, the reverse ought to hold true at the other. Here, however, the willingness to sacrifice profit for volume does not ordinarily find an equal degree of enthusiasm for increasing profits when volume itself is to be sacrificed. Minimum order charges are, in effect, the reverse of a volume discount, but their application and the level at which they are invoked are usually far short of the need. Surprisingly, some fairly large manufacturing companies will be found to have no minimum charge whatsoever. In companies doing perhaps $50 million a year in sales, orders are routinely accepted and shipped at values less than $10. Little thought seems to be given to the combined cost of order entry, inventory control, shipping, and billing that must process the $10 order with the same time and attention to detail required by the $10,000 shipment. Such orders should be referred to distributors if the company has a distributor network. If not, a minimum charge should be made that will at least cover the nuisance value of the small order. And since no precise measurement of the handling cost is really possible, the amount will have to be arbitrary. The decision on how much this should be will depend on many factors—the size of the company, the average unit sales price, the prevailing custom in the industry, and so forth. As an order of magnitude, however, anything below a $50 minimum would seem to be totally inadequate.

Advance Payments

It has been shown that the collection of trade receivables becomes a vital part of the pricing need. If extended terms are offered, both the investment and possibly the risk are increased, cost factors that must be recovered in a higher price. This need is already recognized by many companies in the concept of cash discounts, terms that in effect offer a lower price for earlier payment. As has been noted, however, the payment terms are difficult to enforce; they can lead to disputed deductions on the part of the customer, and in general do not work as intended. The concept is right but the mechanics are often wrong.

A more positive way of accomplishing the same objective is available to some companies—those engaged, for instance, in the manufacture of specialized industrial equipment. Terms that call for a cash deposit with the order are usually acceptable in the trade, but they are not always used to the greatest advantage. An order, for example, for a piece of equipment priced at $100,000 might call for a 25 percent deposit with the order. If delivery is scheduled in three months and the balance of payment is due in 30 days net, the company will have the use of $25,000 cash for a period of four months, an advantage the company can measure in one of two ways.

Invested in money market funds at a prudent 12 percent rate, the *cash flow* of the company will be increased by $1,000 for the four months, equivalent to a 1 percent discount in price. More importantly—and more correctly—capital will have been reduced at a pretax cost of 37 percent a year for an *economic gain* of over $3,000, yielding the equivalent of a 3 percent price reduction. It is the latter measurement, not the former, that management should use in its pricing decisions. And since many customers will cling to the cash flow measurement only, the terms offered will appear most attractive and be found workable.

Returns and Allowances

The sales terms and conditions under this heading usually fall into several categories. First will be returns to stock, returns of salable merchandise, which in effect simply cancel the original transaction and restore the inventory for the next opportunity. The only long-term impact on pricing, assuming that the goods are then resold within a short period of time, will be the handling and clerical expense involved plus the short-term loss of use of money. A firm policy is needed, however, that states clearly the conditions under which such returns may be made and for what period of time. Lack of a clearly defined policy can lead to the eventual erosion of effective prices, with obsolete models or outmoded fashions returned for credit adding up to a sizable discount over time.

A second category is in the area of defective returns and product warranties. The policy required here will depend on the nature of the product, its useful life, and the custom of the industry. It is a pricing factor that may be difficult to control and hence difficult to predict. The very definition of the word "defective" may be subject to varying interpretations, questions leading to disputed claims, delayed payments, and final credit allowances that may have a marked impact on the effective price. When negotiable or acceptable in the trade, a *controlled cost* is often a preferable solution, namely, offering a stated discount in lieu of warranty claims. If the quality reputation is good, the offer will have appeal in a lower net price. For the seller, a known price adjustment will have been locked in and possible unknown costs and disputes avoided.

The third and final category in this group is generally described as *price and policy adjustments,* a catchall for price-reduction credits that do not fall within any stated policy or practice. They are not intended to cover pricing errors in billing, adjustments that should be made at the gross sales level, not as a deduction from income. They are, in fact, a measured result of not having a policy or not adhering to one, the cost of yielding to a disputed quantity or amount. As such, they should be avoided in the first place, but some will inevitably be encountered and must be factored into the basic pricing structure as a cost to be recovered.

Trade Discounts

Where used in business, the trade discount generally represents a discount from a price that the seller never expects to realize in the first place. The practice usually starts with a list price. This is sometimes the suggested retail price that the buyer should charge and other times simply a starting price from which discounts may be negotiated in differing markets or opportunities. Properly classified, then, trade discounts are a device, not an actual price adjustment.

In the same general category, and often confused with it as to impact, is the *dealer discount,* which can serve a very different function. This discount will be found in companies where part of the volume is sold directly to the user and part is sold through dealers who service the individual accounts within their territories. Here the discount is a price concession, a reduction from the price the seller would receive if a direct sale were made. It is a concession in exchange for something else, supposedly a trade-off in cost for a lower price. The ex-

Table 14.

	Direct Sales	*Dealer Sales*	*Total*
Gross Sales	$100,000	$40,000	$140,000
Dealer Discounts	0	10,000	10,000
Net Sales	100,000	30,000	130,000
Direct Cost of Goods Sold	50,000	20,000	70,000
Gross Margin	50,000	10,000	60,000
P/V Ratio	50%	25%	43%
Sales Expense	25,000	0	25,000
Profit Contribution	$ 25,000	$10,000	$ 35,000
Percent to Sales	25%	25%	25%

change is usually seen as a savings in direct sales expense, a reduction in inventories, and a prompt collection of receivables. These are considered in concept, but seldom fully measured in practice, with the result that the discounts do not actually produce the contemplated results.

A typical financial presentation of sales through dealers versus direct sales is shown in Table 14. This presentation shows identical profitability between the two methods of distribution, with the 25 percent dealer discount completely offset by a savings in sales expense. On the basis of this analysis, the company might well proceed to enlarge its dealer network and gradually reduce or even eliminate its own internal sales force.

A different decision, however, might be indicated if a couple of missing measurements were added to the picture, as shown in Table 15. When fully measured, the 72-day average collection of dealer receivables, as measured by the five times turnover of balances due, represents a substantial added price concession compared to the 43-day collection notice for direct accounts. In addition, the consigned stock in dealer inventories is nearly twice the level required per dollar of sales for the accounts handled by the company's own sales force. The dealer sales have, in effect, been given price discounts in three directions at once: first, in a 25 percent discount on the face of the sales invoice; second, in the use of interest-free money for an average of 29 days beyond the normal payment period; and third, in the tie-up of funds in a slow-moving inventory over $5,000 in excess of normal needs.

The total discount can then be computed from a comparison of results measured in terms of the rate of return on assets managed. For the dealer sales to produce a comparable 100 percent return on $18,000 of assets, the contribution would also have to be $18,000 instead of $10,000. The missing $8,000 in contribution on 40,000 of sales amounts to another 20 percent discount in price—truly a hidden discount for companies

Table 15.

	Direct Sales	Dealer Sales	Total
Gross Sales	$100,000	$40,000	$140,000
Profit Contribution	25,000	10,000	35,000
Percent to Sales	25%	25%	25%
Accounts Receivable	12,000	8,000	20,000
Turnover	8.3	5.0	7.0
Inventory	13,000	10,000	23,000
Turnover	7.7	4.0	6.1
Assets Managed	$ 25,000	$18,000	$ 43,000
Turnover	4.0	2.2	3.2
Return on Assets Managed	100.0%	55.5%	81.4%

that fail to measure the net profitability of pricing decisions.

When the total impact of the sales terms and conditions is taken into account, it becomes obvious that the management of pricing goes well beyond the initial step of determining the selling price per unit of volume. Without due regard for each of the factors described, what appeared to be an adequate pricing decision may easily be negated entirely in a series of steps that will erode profitability. Not only do they require careful analysis and reporting in order to guard against their often hidden effect on pricing, but the problem itself should be turned into an area of opportunity. The opportunity will present itself in a decision to gain competitive advantage by not following a general price increase, but by getting the same net effect through changing the sales terms themselves. The first is explicit and highly visible. The second is implicit; if it is not always fully measured by the seller, it is likely to be only dimly perceived by the buyer.

6

Pricing the Service Business

The application of the pricing curve concept to a service business seems to present several obstacles that would make most of the calculations meaningless. First, there is no physical product for which a unit cost can be computed, so that there is nothing tangible to be inventoried and priced. Second, there is usually very little in the way of direct variable costs and expenses related to the sales volume, a factor that would limit, if not eliminate entirely, the use of a direct costing approach. And third, there will be very little value displayed on the balance sheet in the way of total capital employed or of assets managed.

The product will not be a thing but a service, not

Table 16.

Cash	$ 10,000
Accounts Receivable	70,000
Furniture and Equipment	30,000
Other Assets	20,000
Total Assets	$130,000
Payables and Accruals	(15,000)
Capital Employed	$115,000

something physical, but something related to knowl-edge and expertise and based on the passage of time. The costs of the business will be largely fixed as period or time-oriented expenses, such as salaries, rent, and office supplies. And the assets on the balance sheet will be limited to a small amount of working cash, a few supplies in inventory, the furniture and equipment, and the accounts receivable. It will be far from the capital-intensive characteristics of heavy industry and far re-moved from the inventory-intensive requirements of a retail establishment. Unlike these two, the service busi-ness is people-intensive, a category not recognized in generally accepted accounting principles as having any measurable value. In sum, a service business would ap-pear to be completely unsuited to any normal ap-proach to pricing.

If, for example, the total of the capital reported on the accounting form of the balance sheet were to be used as a base for calculating the profit requirement of a small independent accounting firm with revenues of $500,000 a year, the balance sheet would offer as an average base* the figures shown in Table 16.

If the profit requirement were then placed at a need for a pretax return of 40 percent, the targeted profit

*Using average rates found in Annual Statement Studies, 1980 Edi-tion, Robert Morris Associates.

dollars would amount to only $46,000 a year. This would make a strange comparison indeed with the income statement for this same company shown in Table 17.

Something would appear to be wrong with one of the two calculations. Either the profit was abnormally high as a percent of revenue and would not be sustained, or the measurement of capital was too low and something had been left out. Since a review of other firms in the same line of business shows a similar profit-to-revenue comparison, the first possibility must be ruled out. And since a pretax return of over 100 percent on the capital employed in any business is not too likely a result, the problem narrows down to the measurement of capital, not as a question of valuation of the elements reported but as a question of values left out.

The accounting form of the balance sheet is limited to the measurement of financial assets and liabilities and to the monetary book value of physical things, such as inventory, machines, and equipment. In a service business, therefore, *it does not provide for measuring the total assets required to provide the service,* to provide the basic revenue of the business. The missing element is, of course, the value of people, an intangible asset in one sense, but a very fundamental source of earning power.

Table 17.

Revenue	$500,000
Operating Expenses	375,000
Pretax Profit	$125,000
Percent Return on Revenue	25.0%
Capital Employed	$115,000
Turnover	4.35
Pretax Return on Capital	109%

In a service business, such as medicine, law, or accounting, people are not only an asset missing from the valuation of capital, they are in fact the entire principal asset of the business. They are susceptible to valuation and measurement, but to do so obviously requires a departure from normal accounting procedures.

Formulas have been proposed for "human resource accounting," formulas that take into account such factors as age, education, and experience together with total compensation as a framework to determine an imputed asset value of the professional. It is imprecise but certainly worthy of the effort, since there is undoubtedly a value to be measured and a substantial one at that. Since the need exists and no better way has been found to meet it, a rough approximation is preferable to ignoring the problem entirely. The approximated value will be neither precise nor provable, but then neither are many of the accounted values already listed on the balance sheet.

Heavy manufacturing has been described as capital intensive, retailing as inventory intensive, and the types of service business just discussed as people intensive. There is another type of service business that requires a still different classification—one that might be described as franchise intensive—where the principal asset of the business lies in the exclusivity granted by a franchise, a permit, or a license. Such assets clearly create earning power and in some instances also have an inherent market value.

In the operation of a radio station, for example, the principal asset will be found in the value of the license granted by the Federal Communications Commission. The special needs of this industry, where time becomes the inventory and a government permit the principal asset, have been met in a presentation of programmed instruction prepared by the author for one of the largest radio rep firms in the United States, McGavren Guild, Inc. of New York. Published originally as an added service to its client stations, it is reproduced here in its entirety with permission of the copyright owner.

The original mailing to radio station managers throughout the country included the following message from Ralph Guild, president of the firm:

In today's media arena, the health of a radio station can be judged by the mind of the manager who operates it. His objective shouldn't be just to sell spots, but to devise an integrated pricing system that will have, as its ultimate goal, the overall improvement of the profitability of the station he manages.

In an attempt to properly determine those radio station rate card pricing policies that will deliver a greater degree of station profitability, the radio industry is in the process of replacing the "professional broadcaster" with the "professional broadcasting businessman."

The professional broadcaster has been one who has always looked at the industry and the pricing policy of his own station in a somewhat traditional sense. He has historically based his decisions on "what we've always done," "what the market will bear," or "what the competitor down the street is doing." Unhappily, these external methods of pricing have little to do with a station's real "internal" needs of establishing a rate card policy that reflects a true picture of required cashflow and profit.

As a result, when the final year-end tally is taken, the station manager has often been unable to determine just where he was, or how he got there in the first place. All he knows is that he did better or worse than the year before. He can sigh with relief if he's been able to pay his bills and return a slight profit to his investors. Or he can hopelessly hang his head if the creditors start knocking.

The professional broadcasting businessman, on the other

hand, understands that station managements must take the time to give a hard and factual look at their own projected operating costs, the gross billings they expect to achieve, the potential annual inventory they have on hand to release, and their station assets and liabilities. Putting these items in proper order, this new breed of manager can readily determine what his station's pricing structure should be.

There is an existing method that a manager can use to determine his station's goals for profitability, that can prejudge real profit potential, and that can aid the manager in assessing and structuring genuine financial growth on a simple formulated basis. The demand for such a method is so acute, that we, at McGavren Guild, are planning a series of industry seminars throughout the coming year in order to make this information available.

Understanding "Pricing Your Radio Station For Profit" doesn't require great financial expertise. The facts are easily come by, and the formulas are logical. The key is an approach which includes a total calculation of the costs of doing business (including the costs of assets employed) at various levels of capacity, i.e., the number of minutes sold versus the total number of minutes of advertising time available for sale during the year. The selling price is then determined based on the recovery of total costs or the rate of return the station management requires on its investment.

In summary, the profitable pricing of a service business must be based on a valuation of capital that includes all the assets actually employed. For a radio station, it will be the value of the license that must be added to the balance sheet; for other types of services, the human factor will have the greater value. These can be left out, but only at the risk of prices and earnings that will prove inadequate to replace them.

pricing your radio station for profit

preface

This booklet has been prepared in the belief that it will assist you — the Station Manager — in pricing your radio time for improved profits.

Pricing has always been a critical part of the management job, and with the prospect of continuing inflation and rising costs, it may well become the most vital part of your financial planning and control for the future.

McGavren—Guild is pleased to provide this guide as one additional tool in our program of acting for you as a full service rep company.

As a first step in improving the profitability of your radio station, we believe you will find it worthwhile to prepare your monthly and year-to-date operating statements in a somewhat different form than the one usually presented by the accounting process alone.

The format we believe you will find the most useful simply segregates the fixed and variable costs of doing business as shown · in the following example:

SUGGESTED FORM OF OPERATING STATEMENT
(DOLLARS IN THOUSANDS)

	Year Ending
Number Minutes Sold	90,000
Average Price Per Minute	$ 20.00
Gross Billing	$ 1,800
Less — Agency Commissions	220
Net Billing	1,580
Direct Variable Costs:	
Rep. Commissions, Royalties, Bad Debts, etc.	230
Gross Margin	1,350
Gross Margin % of Gross Billing	75%
Period Expenses:	
Program	300
Technical	70
Selling	100
Depreciation	30
General & Administrative	300
Total Period Expenses	800
Pretax Profit	550
Provision for Federal Income Tax	250
Net Earnings After Taxes	$ 300

You will note that this statement measures the percentage of Gross Margin to Gross Billing. Since the variable costs of commissions, royalties and the like are a fairly constant percentage of volume, the resulting Gross Margin percentage is also a constant percentage which will hold true at any level of volume. Secondly, the Period Expenses — often called the "Fixed Overhead" — are grouped and identified as the supporting cost of being in business — a cost which will change only in incremental steps over the entire range of volume.

The resulting measurement on the "bottom line" — the Net Earnings After Taxes — however, is only one-half of the measurement you will need to determine the true profitability of operations. It must next be linked up with a statement of the Capital Employed which produced the earnings — a final measurement of the "rate of return."

For this next step, you will need to bring forward a measurement of Capital Employed — a value normally found on the Balance Sheet. A typical Balance Sheet which might tie-in with the preceding Operating Statement, however, would probably look something like the following:

TYPICAL BALANCE SHEET
(DOLLARS IN THOUSANDS)

Assets:		Liabilities:	
Cash	$ 50	Accounts Payable	$ 50
Accounts Receivable — Net	300	Accrued Payroll and Expenses	100
Land, Buildings and Equipment — Net of Depreciation	360	Total Operating Debt	150
Prepaid Expenses, Goodwill and Other Misc. Assets	90	Capital Employed:	
		Common Equity	650
Total Assets	$800	Total Liabilities & Net Worth	$800

93

In other words, it will not include the most important capital value actually used in operating your station — the asset value of the station itself, a value usually far greater than the combined book value of the accounted assets and capital listed on the Balance Sheet.

This value can be determined by appraisal and should be included in your measurement of total Capital Employed if you are to get a true statement of the profitability of earnings

For purposes of demonstration, we will assume an appraisal asset value of the station to be $3.7 million. The calculation should then be made as follows:

Net Earnings After Taxes		$ 300
Net Book Capital	$ 650	
Appraisal Asset Value of Station	3,700	
Total Capital Employed		$4,350
Net Return on Capital		6.9%

The next step is to determine what the rate of return should be for true profitability. And since "what it should be" is the rate of return the investor expects as compensation for risk, the answer can be quantified by comparison with rates of return offered by alternate choices of investment. With the current and anticipated interest rates available on bank deposits, treasury bills, saving certificates and the like — all of which present a considerably lower degree of risk — the current requirements for risk capital in your station can be considered as a 20% net return after taxes — a rate of return which should be regarded as the cost of capital employed.

To now carry this objective rate of return forward into the pricing calculations you will need, you will next find it useful to translate the net after-tax return on total capital employed into a pre-tax rate of return on the "Assets Managed" — namely, the Asset Value of the Station and the net balance of the Accounts Receivable.

This can be done as follows:

Total Capital Employed	$4,350
20% Return Required	870
Pre-Tax Profit Required	1,600
Assets Managed:	
Asset Value of Station	3,700
Net Accounts Receivable	300
Total Assets Managed	$4,000
Pre-Tax Profit Required as	
% of Assets Managed	40%

With this brief background of reasoning and measurement, you are now ready to use these tools in the most important area of your business management — pricing your station for profit.

pricing

step 1

Determine the total number of minutes of advertising time you have available for sale during the year. This should be based on your total operating hours for the year, and the number of minutes available for sale becomes your measure of "capacity".

step 2

Next, construct a worksheet in which you can enter some values at five different levels of capacity. If, for example, you have determined an annual capacity of 150,000 minutes — the worksheet would be set up as follows:

PRICE/VOLUME ANALYSIS
(DOLLARS IN THOUSANDS)

% Utilization of Capacity →	20%	40%	60%	80%	100%
Minutes Available for Sale	30,000	60,000	90,000	120,000	150,000

step 3

Determine your present utilization of capacity — i.e., how many minutes of time you are currently selling versus the total time available for sale. To illustrate, we will assume the present level to be 90,000 minutes a year or 60% of capacity.

step 4

Using the worksheet you have set up, next enter the value of Assets Managed at the present 60% level of capacity as follows:

PRICE/VOLUME ANALYSIS
(DOLLARS IN THOUSANDS)

% Utilization of Capacity →	20%	40%	60%	80%	100%
Minutes Available for Sale	30,000	60,000	90,000	120,000	150,000
Assets Managed:					
Capital Asset Value			$ 3,700		
Accounts Receivable — Net			300		
Total Assets Managed			$ 4,000		

step 5

Next, compute a pre-tax profit requirement equal to 40% of the total value of Assets Managed:

PRICE/VOLUME ANALYSIS
(DOLLARS IN THOUSANDS)

% Utilization of Capacity $\longrightarrow$	20%	40%	60%	80%	100%
Minutes Available for Sale	30,000	60,000	90,000	120,000	150,000
Assets Managed:					
Capital Asset Value			$ 3,700		
Accounts Receivable – Net			300		
Total Assets Managed			$ 4,000		
Profit Before Taxes Required @ 40% Return on Assets			$ 1,600		

step 6

Now list the present level of Period Expenses or fixed overhead that you will have to recover in your pricing:

PRICE/VOLUME ANALYSIS
(DOLLARS IN THOUSANDS)

% Utilization of Capacity ⟶	20%	40%	60%	80%	100%
Minutes Available for Sale	30,000	60,000	90,000	120,000	150,000
Assets Managed:					
Capital Asset Value			$ 3,700		
Accounts Receivable – Net			300		
Total Assets Managed			$ 4,000		
Profit Before Taxes Required @					
40% Return on Assets			$ 1,600		
Add: Period Expenses:					
Program			300		
Technical			70		
Selling			100		
Depreciation			30		
General & Administrative			300		
Total Period Expenses			800		

step 7

Add the total of your Period Expenses to the total of the pre-tax profit dollars required. This will give you the dollars of Gross Margin required at the 60% level of capacity:

PRICE/VOLUME ANALYSIS
(DOLLARS IN THOUSANDS)

% Utilization of Capacity →	20%	40%	60%	80%	100%
Minutes Available for Sale	30,000	60,000	90,000	120,000	150,000
Assets Managed:					
Capital Asset Value			$ 3,700		
Accounts Receivable — Net			300		
Total Assets Managed			$ 4,000		
Profit Before Taxes Required @					
40% Return on Assets			$ 1,600		
Add: Period Expenses:					
Program			300		
Technical			70		
Selling			100		
Depreciation			30		
General & Administrative			300		
Total Period Expenses			800		
Gross Margin Required			2,400		

step 8

Divide the Gross Margin dollars by your Gross Margin percentage to Gross Billing (75% in this example) as shown on your current operating statement. This will give you the total dollars of Gross Billing required at this level of operations:

PRICE/VOLUME ANALYSIS
(DOLLARS IN THOUSANDS)

% Utilization of Capacity⟶	20%	40%	60%	80%	100%
Minutes Available for Sale	30,000	60,000	90,000	120,000	150,000
Assets Managed:					
Capital Asset Value			$ 3,700		
Accounts Receivable — Net			300		
Total Assets Managed			$ 4,000		
Profit Before Taxes Required @					
40% Return on Assets			$ 1,600		
Add: Period Expenses:					
Program			300		
Technical			70		
Selling			100		
Depreciation			30		
General & Administrative			300		
Total Period Expenses			800		
Gross Margin Required			2,400		
Gross Margin ÷ 75% = Gross Billing Required			3,200		

step 9

Now divide the Gross Billing dollars required by the number of minutes sold to find the average price per minute needed to meet your profit target:

PRICE/VOLUME ANALYSIS
(DOLLARS IN THOUSANDS)

%Utilization of Capacity ⟶	20%	40%	60%	80%	100%
Minutes Available for Sale	30,000	60,000	90,000	120,000	150,000
Assets Managed:					
Capital Asset Value			$ 3,700		
Accounts Receivable — Net			300		
Total Assets Managed			$ 4,000		
Profit Before Taxes Required @					
40% Return on Assets			$ 1,600		
Add: Period Expenses:					
Program			300		
Technical			70		
Selling			100		
Depreciation			30		
General & Administrative			300		
Total Period Expenses			800		
Gross Margin Required			2,400		
Gross Margin ÷ 75% = Gross Billing Required			3,200		
Average Price Per Minute Required			$ 35.50		

101

step 10

Next, compute your breakeven price. To do this, subtract the dollars of profit required from the total Gross Billing to find the level of volume that will result in zero profit. Divide this figure by the number of minutes sold to determine the breakeven price per minute.

PRICE/VOLUME ANALYSIS
(DOLLARS IN THOUSANDS)

% Utilization of Capacity ⟶	20%	40%	60%	80%	100%
Minutes Available for Sale	30,000	60,000	90,000	120,000	150,000
Assets Managed:					
Capital Asset Value			$ 3,700		
Accounts Receivable — Net			300		
Total Assets Managed			$ 4,000		
Profit Before Taxes Required @ 40% Return on Assets			$ 1,600		
Add: Period Expenses:					
Program			300		
Technical			70		
Selling			100		
Depreciation			30		
General & Administrative			300		
Total Period Expenses			800		
Gross Margin Required			2,400		
Gross Margin ÷ 75% = Gross Billing Required			3,200		
Price Per Minute Required			$ 35.50		

Gross Billing Required		$ 3,200
Less — Profit Requirement		1,600
Breakeven Gross Billing		1,600
Average Breakeven Price Per Minute		$ 17.75

step 11

Now repeat steps four through ten at each of the four remaining levels of capacity — 20%, 40%, 80% and 100%. In doing this, it is critical that you carefully put your own judgement on the level of assets required at each step of capacity as well as the level of Period Expense support required. Do not use ratios or a formula approach since the only constants in your calculations will be (a) the 40% required return on Assets Managed, and (b) the Gross Margin percentage to Gross Billing:

PRICE/VOLUME ANALYSIS
(DOLLARS IN THOUSANDS)

% Utilization of Capacity ⟶	20%	40%	60%	80%	100%
Minutes Available for Sale	30,000	60,000	90,000	120,000	150,000
Assets Managed:					
Capital Asset Value	$ 3,700	$ 3,700	$ 3,700	$ 3,700	$ 3,700
Accounts Receivable — Net	200	250	300	350	400
Total Assets Managed	$ 3,900	$ 3,950	$ 4,000	$ 4,050	$ 4,100

Profit Before Taxes Required @ 40% Return on Assets	$ 1,560	$ 1,580	$ 1,600	$ 1,620	$ 1,640
Add: Period Expenses:					
Program	200	250	300	320	340
Technical	50	60	70	80	90
Selling	90	90	100	110	120
Depreciation	30	30	30	30	30
General & Administrative	230	260	300	300	300
Total Period Expenses	600	690	800	840	880
Gross Margin Required	2,160	2,270	2,400	2,460	2,520
Gross Margin ÷ 75% = Gross Billing Required	2,880	3,030	3,200	3,280	3,360
Price Per Minute Required	$ 96.00	$ 50.40	$ 35.50	$ 27.30	$ 22.40
Gross Billing Required	$ 2,880	$ 3,030	$ 3,200	$ 3,280	$ 3,360
Less – Profit Requirement	1,560	1,580	1,600	1,620	1,640
Breakeven Gross Billing	1,320	1,450	1,600	1,660	1,720
Breakeven Price Per Minute	$ 44.00	$ 24.20	$ 17.75	$ 13.80	$ 11.45

step 12

Your worksheet is now completed, and you have developed two sets of pricing figures — the first, a set of prices at five different levels of capacity that, if used, would produce a constant rate of a 40% pre-tax return on Assets Managed. The second, a set of prices that will produce only breakeven results on your operating statement.

step 13

Finally, post these prices on a Pricing Curve which will link up the prices required at both the profit level and the breakeven level — providing a measurement which will now allow you to determine the pricing required at any intermediate level of capacity.

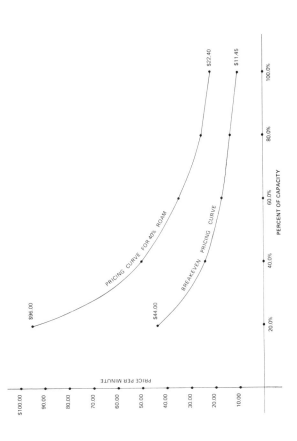

step 14

Finally enter your current level of volume and price on the Pricing Curve to show where you now stand in relation to your own target.

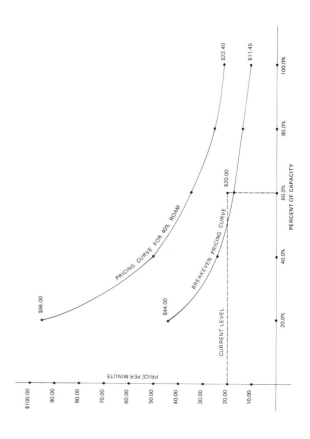

step 15

Using the Pricing Curve as a financial tool for planning and control, your objective is now to set a pricing strategy that will yield profitable results at an optimum use of capacity. The curve will serve as a guideline or bench-mark to tell you the price required — how low you can afford to go to get more volume — and where the stopping point will be. And remember that a better collection of receivables and/or a reduction in fixed overhead will also serve to reduce the need for higher prices. The management of price thus becomes the total management of volume, cost and investment.

WORKSHEET
PRICE/VOLUME ANALYSIS
(DOLLARS IN THOUSANDS)

% Utilization of Capacity ⟶	%		%		%		%		%
Minutes Available for Sale									
Assets Managed:									
Capital Asset Value	$		$		$		$		$
Accounts Receivable — Net									
Total Assets Managed	$		$		$		$		$
Profit Before Taxes Required @									
40% Return on Assets	$		$		$		$		$
Add: Period Expenses:									
Program									
Technical									
Selling									
Depreciation									
General & Administrative									
Total Period Expenses									

107

	Gross Margin Required				
Gross Margin ÷ 75% = Gross Billing Required	$	$	$	$	$
Price Per Minute Required	$	$	$	$	$
Gross Billing Required	$	$	$	$	$
Less — Profit Requirement					
Breakeven Gross Billing	$	$	$	$	$
Breakeven Price Per Minute					

7

Bidding
the Construction Job

The construction company presents another new set of problems in pricing its product. Unlike the manufacturing business, it has no planned production of a product mix and no measurement of the cost per unit of output. And unlike the radio station, it has no constant use of physical assets or exclusive license to do business. It represents a series of new ventures, with each separate job becoming a new business by itself, with its own use of assets, its own estimated life to completion, and its own individual risk.

Its capacity tends to be a much more flexible measurement, not determined solely by time limitations, as in the case of the radio station, or largely by the phys-

ical limitations of space, equipment, materials, or man-
power, as noted for manufacturing. In most instances,
the two most critical factors determining the capacity
of construction—equipment and labor—are in themselves quite flexible. Equipment can be leased as required for on-site use, and labor crews are also normally available for hire for the duration of a single job.
The lack of a specified base of capacity thus rules out
the use of the pricing curve, a curve developed from
estimates at different points of a constant capacity measurement.

There is, however, one common thread running
through all three types of business: the *need to recover
the cost of capital employed.* The construction industry will
have its own risk rate, one basically higher than manufacturing, which tends to have more of a continuing
market for its products. The manufacturing risk, in
turn, is higher than that for radio broadcasting, an industry that has more of the aspects of monopoly by
virtue of licenses granted by the Federal Communications Commission. Each industry thus has its own average risk and each business within an industry, its own
individual risk based on its size, reputation, share of
market, and, above all, its record of profitability. Each,
then, has its own cost-of-capital rate as a basic objective
for pricing.

The rate of return required, however, must be applied to a capital base that reflects the total values employed to produce the earnings. And like the radio station, where the value of the station license was not
shown on the typical balance sheet, a substantial asset
value will also be missing from the measurement of
capital for the average construction business. The missing value will consist of two parts: the undervaluation

of assets owned by the company and the value of equipment leased in the various jobs. The problem of undervaluation is one of the many problems created by inflation in the economy and will be dealt with in a later chapter. Leasing can have the same net effect of omitting asset values employed from the capital base, but it is a problem that exists quite apart from inflation and deserves separate treatment on its own.

Leasing

Leasing is a form of debt, perhaps one of the more expensive forms of debt used in business. It has several valid uses in any business. For a company with limited capital, leasing of land, buildings, and equipment may be a virtual necessity, particularly in its early years of growth. For other companies, leasing of computers, for example, may provide greater flexibility for change with a change in technology. Or leasing of a large automotive fleet may be preferable to creating a management function to handle the multitude of decisions concerned with purchasing, insurance, registration, maintenance, and trade-in. Such uses of leasing are indeed valid, as is the temporary use of equipment in the construction business.

The one reason for leasing that is not valid is the one most frequently used in years past: *Companies were not required to account for it on the balance sheet.* The accounting treatment was content to note the use of leasing in a brief footnote to the audit report, a treatment that suggested that leasing was simply an incidental contractual arrangement with no more than a distant relationship to the assets and liabilities reported. It was not surprising, then, that analysts were forced to refer to leasing as a form of "off balance-sheet borrowing," a term as accurate as it was critical of the measurement process.

In more recent times, the accounting profession has taken note of this lack of measurement and has taken steps to correct what it saw as an understatement of liabilities. This move may have met the external needs of financial auditing and banking analysis, but, as with most rules of accounting, the change did very little for the internal needs of management. The rule, issued as Financial Accounting Standards Board (FASB) Rule No. 13, states in part:

A lessee classifies a lease as either a capital lease or an operating lease. If a particular lease meets any one of the following classification criteria, it is a capital lease:

a. The lease transfers ownership of the property to the lessee by the end of the lease term.

b. The lease contains an option to purchase the leased property at a bargain price.

c. The lease term is equal to or greater than 75 percent of the estimated economic life of the leased property.

d. The present value of rental and other minimum lease payments equals or exceeds 90 percent of the fair value of the leased property less any investment tax credit retained by the lessor.

The last two criteria are not applicable when the beginning of the lease term falls within the last 25 percent of the total estimated economic life of the leased property.

The amount to be recorded by the lessee as an asset and an obligation under a capital lease is the lesser of the present value of the rental and other minimum lease payments or the fair value of the leased property. Leased property under a capital lease is amortized in a manner consistent with the lessee's normal depreciation policy for owned assets; the amortization period is restricted to the lease term, rather than the life of the asset, unless the lease provides for transfer of title or includes a bargain purchase option. The periodic rental payments are treated as payments of the lease obligation and as interest expense (principal and interest) so that a constant periodic rate of interest is recorded on the remaining balance of the obligation.

If none of the criteria is met, the lease is classified as an operating lease by a lessee. *Neither an asset nor an obligation is recorded for operating leases.* Rental payments are recorded as rental expense in the income statement in a systematic manner, which is usually straight-line.

Under such a ruling most of the leases for on-site use of equipment in a construction business would be designated as operating leases. Although representing substantial asset value, they would not meet the criteria listed for capitalization and thus would not be given recognition as assets employed to produce the earnings of the business. If followed, this one-sided accounting treatment can have a decidedly detrimental effect on pricing decisions and hence on the ultimate profitability of the enterprise.

The distinction that the accounting rule attempts to create between a capital lease and an operating lease may satisfy the technician's definition of recorded assets and liabilities, but it ignores completely the economic measurement of profit as a required rate of return on investment. And whether the investment used to produce the profit is owned or leased is completely beside the point. It is employed to run the business and as such must be measured as an asset regardless of where title to the property may reside.

The full asset value must be measured for several reasons. First, if it is omitted or understated, the resulting measurements of return on invested capital will be inflated, and will thus not present a true picture of the profitability of the business. Table 18 shows how a financial statement prepared under the accounting rule for so-called operating leases, for example, might appear.

According to this presentation, the company has met its goal of a required rate of return of 20 percent after tax on total capital employed. Everything would appear to be in order, including the pricing formula that had produced the necessary earnings. Not shown, however, is the impact of having used leased equipment with an asset value of $1.5 million during the year, an investment responsible for much of the reported income and accounted earnings. Also not shown is a measurement of the implicit interest factor included in the total of lease expense charged to operations, an amount totaling $300,000 at a derived interest rate of 20 percent per year.

Table 18.

Sales	$10,000,000
Operating Costs	
Materials, Labor, and Overhead	8,550,000
Lease Expense	450,000
Total Cost	9,000,000
Profit before Tax	1,000,000
Tax Provision @ 50%	500,000
Net Earnings	$ 500,000
Capital Employed	
Working Capital	$ 2,000,000
Fixed Capital Owned	500,000
Total Capital	$ 2,500,000
Return on Capital Employed	20.0%

These factors will emerge when the use of leased assets is fully recognized in the financial statements. This involves a series of steps. The first is simply a recognition of the asset value employed, a value supplied by the use of debt in the form of leasing. This value should then be brought on the balance sheet by an accounting entry as follows:

Debit Leased Assets $1,500,000
     Credit Leased Capital $1,500,000

The balance sheet now presents the use of the equipment exactly as if the company had in fact borrowed the money from the bank and purchased the asset directly. The new account, Leased Assets, will be shown on the left-hand side of the balance sheet along with assets that are owned, identifying it simply as another asset of the business, but one to which another party has title. The offsetting credit side of the entry also records an interest-bearing liability of a like amount, a debt to be eliminated upon return of the asset, but one that currently represents a use of the company's borrowing capacity.

The second step required involves recognition of the fact that the total earnings of the business have been understated by the net cost of the implicit interest factor included in the lease payments, a factor representing a distribution of earnings and not an operating expense. This amount can be derived by first determining the depreciation charge that the owner of the equipment—the lessor—has included in the lease cost. Since the asset value itself has already been determined, the amount of depreciation can be extracted as the amount that would be charged if in fact the company had purchased and taken title to the equipment. Once this analysis is made, the interest factor can be derived simply as the difference between the lease expense and the depreciation charge, and a second accounting entry made as follows to correct the presentation of the income statement:

Dr. Depreciation on Leased Assets	$150,000	
Dr. Interest on Leased Capital	300,000	
Cr. Lease Expense		$450,000

The books of account will now present the same set of measurements under leasing as would be recorded for direct borrowing and purchase of the equipment—an economic measurement of asset value employed to run the business. From this adjusted base, a corrected statement can be prepared that presents quite a different picture of profitability—and quite a different appraisal of the pricing process. (See Table 19.)

The full disclosure of the impact of leasing thus shows that the profitability of the business is not a 20 percent return on capital as originally supposed, but only 16.3 percent, considerably short of the target. Understating the total amount of capital employed can thus result in underpricing the product—in this case, in underbidding the construction job. And ultimately, although the effects will be hidden from view by the accounting process, the company will begin a downward spiral of profitability that will eventually impair its ability to do business.

1. The pass through of implicit interest as an operating expense is in effect a zero rate of return on the use of the capital employed via leasing.
2. The company may find it necessary at some point

Table 19.

Sales	$10,000,000
Operating Costs	
Materials, Labor, and Overhead	$ 8,550,000
Depreciation on Leased Assets	150,000
Total	$ 8,700,000
Operating Margin	$ 1,300,000
Interest on Leased Capital	300,000
Profit before Tax	$ 1,000,000
Tax Provision @ 50%	500,000
Net Accounted Profit	$ 500,000
Net Cost of Interest	150,000
Total Net Earnings	$ 650,000
Capital Employed	
Working Capital	$ 2,000,000
Fixed Capital Owned	500,000
Leased Capital	1,500,000
Total Capital	$ 4,000,000
Return on Capital Employed	16.3%

to purchase the assets rather than to lease them. Price levels established under leasing would not be adequate to provide the rate of return required on the new capital.

3. Even if these two factors are ignored, a third exists that eventually cannot be ignored. Leasing is a form of debt, and debt capacity, or the ability to borrow, is based in any business on the strength of the equity. Inadequate earnings will not provide the equity base required in the future, and the ability to borrow in the form of leasing will itself be impaired.

The measurement of the asset base to include leasing thus becomes an important first step in providing a proper base for pricing decisions—a necessary step in any business, but one usually more critical in the construction business, where leasing may account for a larger percentage of total assets employed. It must be followed, however, by a second step of perhaps equal importance before all obstacles to the bidding process can be removed. This step will apply to the bidding process in any type of job-shop operation, to any situation where prices must be quoted under conditions of constant change with respect to product, time, and volume. It has to do with the behavior and measurement of cost itself.

Use of Overhead Rates

The behavior of cost has been noted earlier in the references to direct costing and in examples of costs that respond in a nearly linear fashion to changes in volume as opposed to the group of costs and expenses that demonstrate a behavior pattern independent of short-term fluctuations in volume and that are essentially time oriented or relatively fixed in nature. These two patterns exist in any business, but they are perhaps more evident in a business such as basic manufacturing where sales forecasts and production schedules provide a relatively continuous flow of the input of costs and the output of goods. Here the concept of direct costing is more visible and hence used more frequently than in the job-shop. Most job-shop operations, ranging from the small machine shop to the large construction business, are prone to use absorption costing measurements by applying overhead or burden rates first to the bid itself and second to the recording of performance in carrying out the job. The intent, of course, is to recover that group of costs that cannot be measured individually to each job and to include a factor in each bid as a percentage of labor or a percentage of material cost or both.

Since overhead rates must be based on assumptions of both volume and cost, they are arbitrary, tend to become outdated soon after they are developed, and are frequently discounted as not representing "real costs" by those preparing the bids. This last impression will frequently appear to be completely verified by subsequent financial statements reporting an "overabsorption of burden" as a sort of negative cost or as miscellaneous income for the period. When overhead turns in the opposite direction and becomes underabsorbed, as it inevitably must from time to time, it takes on no greater meaning. Instead of adjusting the overhead rate to conform to the new level of activity, the impact tends to be discounted on the up side and then totally misdirected on the down side.

When reports show that the overhead has been underabsorbed, the impetus should logically be for greater volume aimed at a full recovery of costs. More frequently, however, bids are lowered to take on work that will absorb overhead rather than recover it. Recovering overhead implies a pricing approach that follows a prescribed formula that the company has developed for that purpose, while absorbing overhead implies an arbitrary lowering of the standards in what is generally referred to as marginal pricing. The first is aimed at meeting the targeted profit percent to sales for the period; the second is designed only to produce incremental volume somewhere above the breakeven point. Both, however, have one thing in common—they have been targeted only for a measure of operating profit as a percentage of the sales volume. Neither has been developed to cover the cost of capital employed.

The Bidding Formula

The use of overhead rates for labor and materials carries with it the assumption that the sum of these various elements equals the "total cost" of the product or service. For a manufactured product, the so-called total cost will usually represent only the total *manufacturing* cost, an amount to which must be added factors for selling and administrative expenses before a markup for profit is computed. In the job-shop or construction business, a single overhead factor may be used to cover all the general or indirect costs, leading up to the same assumed base of total estimated cost before profit. The final step in either case is to add a factor for profit to arrive at the price to be bid or quoted for the job. This is usually done in one of two ways, either by dividing the "total cost" by a percentage to determine the price or by multiplying by a percentage to reach the same goal.

If, for example, a profit goal of 20 percent pretax return on sales is set as a pricing target on a computed "total cost" of $800, the two methods would work as shown in Table 20. Of the two, the use of a divisor is the more certain method, since the 80 percent factor relates directly to the 20 percent goal and is readily identified by the person preparing the bid. When a multiplier is used, the assumption is frequently made that adding 20 percent to the cost will yield a 20 percent profit. It obviously will not, but there is persistent difficulty in understanding the point, and many jobs

Table 20.

	Divisor	Multiplier
"Total Cost"	$ 800	$ 800
Factor	80%	125%
Bid Price	1,000	1,000
Accounted Profit	200	200
Profit Percent to Sales	20%	20%

are underbid on this single factor alone. And while this can lead to significant differences in the measurement of operating results, the differences may be completely insignificant when compared to the factor missing in both calculations. Assuming that the calculations are done properly in arriving at the profit factor, two different jobs might be bid as given in Table 21. Both jobs are estimated to last for one year, and both have been bid using a burden rate of 40 percent of labor to cover all indirect costs and expenses. If both bids are successful and if all cost estimates are met, the company expects to realize a profit on each one equal to 20 percent of sales. Management thus views the two bids as being equal in cost, and equal in markup and planned profitability. It is therefore somewhat concerned to find that

Table 21.

	Job A	Job B
Materials	$ 70,000	$ 390,000
Labor	500,000	250,000
Depreciation of Leased Equipment	30,000	60,000
Overhead	200,000	100,000
Total Cost	800,000	800,000
Markup	80%	80%
Bid	$1,000,000	$1,000,000

it has been an unsuccessful bidder on Job A and, at the same time, by far the lowest bidder on Job B—a job that it will later find to be far less than profitable.

What the company has yet to learn is that its formula for pricing did not provide for the recovery of all costs, since no provision was made for the cost of capital employed—a factor that varied widely between the two bids. It was also not aware that targeting for a constant 20 percent pretax rate of return on sales would prove excessive in one instance and inadequate in another. These facts were finally brought to light when a complete analysis of the two bids was prepared, linking the projected operating results with the required investment in capital employed on each bid. (See Table 22.)

Calculations involving the estimated amount of capital to be employed on each bid were relatively easy to make but had been neglected entirely in the preoccupation with applied burden rates and markup of the total operating costs. It was estimated that Accounts Receivable would be collected in approximately 30 days, that a little over two and one-half months' supply of materials would be carried in inventory, and finally that the asset value of equipment to be leased would be depreciated on a straight-line basis over a ten-year estimated life. When these values were added to the picture, two things became immediately evident:

1. With a capital turnover of 2.5, the targeted return on sales of 20 percent resulted in overbidding Job A by a substantial margin. If the required profitability were targeted at a net after-tax return on capital of 20 percent, a pretax return should have been placed at 40 percent,

Table 22.

	Job A	Job B
Operating Costs		
Materials	$ 70,000	$ 390,000
Labor	500,000	250,000
Depreciation of Leased Equipment	30,000	60,000
Overhead	200,000	100,000
Total Cost	$ 800,000	$ 800,000
Markup	80%	80%
Bid	$1,000,000	$1,000,000
Pretax Profit	200,000	200,000
Profit Percent to Sales	20%	20%
Capital Employed		
Accounts Receivable	$ 85,000	$ 85,000
Inventory	15,000	85,000
Leased Equipment	300,000	600,000
Total Capital	$ 400,000	$ 770,000
Turnover	2.5	1.3
Pretax Return on Capital	50.0%	26.0%
Net Return after Tax	25.0%	13.0%

a result that would call for no more than a 16 percent pretax profit on sales when combined with the capital turnover of 2.5 times a year. This would have placed the bid at a little over $952,000 instead of at $1 million, and the bid would presumably have been more competitive.

2. The same pretax return of 40 percent on capital employed on Job B at a turnover rate of only 1.3 times a year would have required a rate of return on sales before tax of approximately 30 percent, not the constant rate of 20 percent called for in the markup of operating costs.

One bid was lost because of overstating the markup required, and the other was won at a rate of return sub-

stantially below the level required for profitable operations. Both mistakes could have been avoided with a
simple redirection of the bidding process, one that starts
with the basic objective of pricing for return on capital
rather than for return on sales.

ROAM Bidding

The cost of capital must be included in the bid price
if the job is to prove profitable in the economic sense
of the measurement. Since only the total enterprise can
be measured in terms of return on capital, that objective must be translated into a subordinate goal that can
be applied to a profit center of activity within the company. As has been shown in an earlier chapter, this
translates under direct costing concepts to a Return on
Assets Managed, a stand-alone requirement of profitability totally devoid of any allocations of common cost
or common investment. Abbreviated as ROAM, the required rate of return at this level of measurement then
becomes the pricing base for the product or service
identified with the profit center. For manufactured
products, it serves as a base for developing the pricing
curve, a technique that shows the price levels required
at various levels of a predetermined capacity. The pricing curve works well in such a situation since the total
need for capital is determined ahead of time and will
vary only in a calculated series of increments over the
total range of volume. The pricing need is thus primarily concerned not with changing investment, but
with changing utilization of the investment.

Job-shop operations basically reverse this situation
with a more flexible measurement of capacity and a

constantly changing use of capital. The same estimate of total capital needs for the year must be made as it is for the manufacturing company, but the use of the investment will not apply evenly to periodic levels of production. On the contrary, it will apply quite unevenly in a wide range of concentration from job to job. This pattern of behavior in the need for capital dictates an approach to bidding that avoids the assumption of common cost inherent in the use of burden rates in favor of a method that emphasizes the changing need for assets managed. This basic difference can perhaps best be illustrated by looking at an actual bid made by a large construction company.

The bid in question involved the construction of a large pipeline for water supply, a job that was to last well over a year. It was bid on the basis of applied overhead rates, plus a markup for profit. (See Table 23.)

In this process, overhead has been computed at 40 percent of direct labor and other variable cost only, on the assumption that it should not apply to the cost of materials or subcontracts. This pass through of costs has ignored the fact that, in dealing with nearly $8 mil-

Table 23.

Direct Labor	$ 640,700
Other Variable Costs	315,300
Materials	7,590,400
Subcontracts	375,100
Direct Variable Costs	$8,921,500
Overhead	382,400
Depreciation of Leased Equipment	178,500
Total Estimated Cost	$9,482,400
Markup	379,200
Bid	$9,861,600

lion of invoices and deliveries, additional operating expenses are likely to be incurred in such areas as purchasing and receiving, handling and storage, and accounting and billing. It has been ignored on the premise that nothing is added to the value of materials or subcontracts in the process and that it would be counterproductive to pyramid the costs by adding overhead to the purchase price itself.

This same attitude was then carried forward in the bidding process when all the calculations reached the point of adding a markup for profit. Here again, the markup was based on the total estimated cost, excluding the costs of materials and subcontracts—a markup of 25 percent on the total operating costs and expenses, intended to yield a pretax profit rate of 20 percent on the internal costs of the job. The fact that it amounted to a markup of only 4 percent on the total estimated cost of nearly $9.5 million and provided a profit rate of only 3.8 percent on the total bid did not appear significant at the time. The bid was entered, and in due course the results were announced, with the company as low bidder by a considerable margin:

Bidder	Amount Bid
1	$ 9,861,600
2	10,245,000
3	10,680,000
4	11,045,000
5	11,130,000
6	11,215,000
7	11,240,000
8	11,295,000
9	11,325,000
10	11,362,000

The company was, of course, gratified to learn of its winning bid, but it was also somewhat disturbed to discover that its bid was more than 10 percent below the average of the other nine bidders and nearly $400,000 below the second lowest bid. Had the job been underestimated? Had some error been made in the calculations? A review of the entire bid process answered both questions in the negative, assuring that the bid had been prepared in the normal fashion.

About this time, however, a new and as of then untried concept was suggested to the company, that of inverting the bidding process and using a targeted ROAM as the point of departure in arriving at the price to be quoted. The company had already adopted the use of the ROAM measurements in its financial reports on an after-the-fact basis, but it was frankly skeptical of the tool as a means of preparing a bid. To test the concept, however, the bid was redone using a ROAM approach in the following manner.

The first step was to determine the ROAM percentage required to provide full profitability for the company at a net 20 percent return after taxes on total average capital employed. This was done in the manner described earlier, by inverting the financial statement and working from the objective back to the input level required to reach it. This developed a ROAM requirement of a 91 percent contribution rate, a measurement of performance to be found in the financial reports after the fact, but a target to be used in bidding the job.

The next step was to determine all the various pieces of equipment to be used on the job and to estimate their current replacement value. Equipment that the company owned and equipment that the company planned to lease for the job were treated alike, since they were recognized as assets to be employed on the job regardless of ownership. It was then necessary to determine how long each piece of equipment would be in use during the life of the job, with estimates varying from approximately six months on some items to nearly two years on others. Using elapsed time rather than operating time as the basis for calculating the use of each asset provided a motivation for the most efficient schedule possible, one with little tolerance for idle time.

When all these factors had been determined, they were brought together to calculate the contribution required on the equipment assets to be employed—the beginning point of the bid. (See Table 24.)

In total this amounted to an average use of equipment amounting to some $660,000 in value for a period of about 13 months. It represented an investment—albeit a temporary one to some extent—whose use must be paid for if true profitability were to be achieved. The computed cost of employing this capital amounted to $647,447 *in addition to* the variable costs of operating the equipment that had been included in the bid.

The cost of capital employed on the job, however, would not be limited to the equipment assets alone,

Table 24.

Equipment Item	Asset Value	91% ROAM	Weeks Usage	Contribution Required
A	$277,000	$252,070	54	$261,765
B	136,000	123,760	50	119,000
C	62,000	56,420	49	53,165
D	48,000	43,680	92	77,280
E	2,500	2,275	48	2,100
F	5,000	4,550	99	8,662
G	74,000	67,340	25	32,375
H	56,000	50,960	95	93,100
Total	$660,500	$601,055	56	$647,447

Table 25.

Item	Monthly Average	ROAM @ 91%	Months Employed	Contribution Required
Retainage	$2,000,000	$1,820,000	4	$606,666
Receivables	720,000	655,200	6	327,600
Inventory	500,000	455,000	5	189,583
Payables	(400,000)	(364,000)	18	(546,000)
Total	$2,820,000	$2,566,200	2.3	$577,849

since an almost equal investment had to be made in the level of working capital required for the job. It was expected, for example, that approximately 20 percent of the contract price would be held as retainage, a tie-up of funds that would not be released until the job had been completed. On the other hand, it was believed that current billings for progress payments as the work moved along could be collected in an average of about 26 days, and a further tie-up of capital in the form of accounts receivable was estimated on this basis. Next, the schedule for the purchase and use of materials on the job indicated an investment in inventory of $500,000 for an average period of five months during the contract. Finally, as an offset to assets committed to the job, an estimate of accounts payable and accrued expenses was placed at an average balance of $400,000 for a period of 18 months. Together, these elements made up another layer of capital to be paid for, a cost that could also be computed at a 91 percent rate of return required. (See Table 25.)

At this point, all the calculations had been made to put the final bid together. It would no longer be necessary to deal with an applied burden rate on any element of cost, be it labor, material, or total operating cost, since the entire overhead itself—or more specifically the total period expenses of the business—had already been locked into the 91 percent ROAM required to recover them. Second, no markup or profit factor would have to be added to the estimated total cost, since the entire profit requirement was also inherent in the 91 percent ROAM required. The markup had, in effect, been put on the assets employed rather than on the operating cost. The final preparation of the bid then proved to be simplicity itself. The estimated total direct variable cost was first brought foward intact from the original bid, and the profit contribution required at the 91 percent ROAM was added to it to yield the price to be bid:

Total Direct Variable Cost	$ 8,921,500
Contribution Required	
On Equipment Assets	647,447
On Working Capital	577,849
Amount to Bid	$10,146,796

Two things emerged from the ROAM bid. First, the company could have increased its bid by some $285,000 and still have been low bidder. More importantly for the future, the process ensured that the cost of capital would be included in all bids, another way of saying that the process would produce a price level adequate to yield the required return on investment. By putting the capital intensity of each bid into full perspective, the ROAM bid will serve to avoid many extremes of overbidding one job and underbidding another. It will not, quite obviously, ensure that all bids are successful. It does provide, however, a measured point of departure in placing the final judgment on what to bid after all the computations have been made.

8

Pricing under Inflation

The needs for a measured approach to pricing have been described for various types of business ventures. They have varied in the step-by-step process of determining the price required, but those needs have all been based on a common concept: the assumption of a system of values and measurements that could be relied on to remain constant, providing a consistent and uniform interpretation of results. In an economy of zero inflation, such constancy could indeed be relied on and attention could be focused on the tactical approaches to pricing rather than on the strategic assumptions determining the need.

Inflation in the monetary system—or more specifically the inflation in the supply of credit throughout the banking system—has severe and widespread effects. Aside from the more visible effect of increases in the general price level, the impact on society includes the destruction of savings, the loss of jobs, and a deterioration of moral values. By destroying the value system, inflation destroys the belief in the work ethic.

Business is by no means immune to the disease of eroding values. It experiences all the ills inflicted on society in general and adds its own particular set of problems to the list. These particular problems arise in three different areas of measurement simultaneously: the measurement of cost, the valuation of capital, and the adequacy of profit. Taken together, they have a compounding effect on the pricing process.

The Measurement of Cost

The measurement of cost is the first and certainly the most highly visible of these three problem areas. By driving the value of the currency down, inflation is exerting an equal and opposite reaction in driving prices up, an inevitable consequence. Thus with rapid and continuing increases in the rate of inflation, it is not surprising that recorded costs are no longer representative of economic values. They are no longer meaningful, since they cannot be repeated in the future and have, in fact, become obsolete almost in the very process of accounting for them. Acquisition cost in its historical sense becomes irrelevant in the measurement system and must be replaced with a new approach to the recognition of cost. It must be a recognition that will deal with the future, not with the past, simply because the values of the past will not be repeated or found again in the future.

Specifically, cost measurement under inflation must be based on *estimated replacement cost,* what the cost is expected to be in the next transaction, not what was recorded in the last one. In some areas of cost, inflation itself will take care of the need for current measurement. In others, the need will be obscured and will require special treatment. This difference can best be seen if a typical income statement is visualized in its usual form, starting with the revenue from sales on the top line and ending with a statement of net accounted profit at the bottom. Taken in order of appearance, each segment can then be analyzed as to any hidden impact of inflation.

Starting from the top, it is safe to say that the sales account itself should present no problem in current measurement, that it has no hidden impact from inflation. If prices have been raised to offset rising costs, management is well aware of the degree of change. Comparisons can also be made against budgets and forecasts or against the volume for a prior period, and unit shipments can provide a test of growth in real terms. While not always precise, the measurement should be adequate and not require adjustment or change in measurement.

The costs and expenses that follow on the income statement present a mixed situation and must be separated into two distinct categories. The first group will be those costs and expenses that flow directly to the income statement as incurred, permitting an immediate measurement of the impact of inflation on the amounts reported. This group will normally include engineering, selling, and general administrative expenses for salaries, travel, supplies, and the like. Where a system of direct costing is also in effect, the period costs of manufacturing are also expensed as incurred, a process that again provides an immediate evaluation of the effects of inflation in terms of rising costs. Comparison to budgets or prior periods will again ensure that no hidden factors are present.

The problem in measurement is confined to the second group of costs—those that originate on the balance sheet as assets and that subsequently flow from the balance sheet to the income statement as costs and expenses. These include the cost of goods sold, which flows from the inventory account, and depreciation, which flows from the fixed asset group of buildings, machinery, equipment, and the like.

When inventory is first acquired or produced, the cost goes directly to the balance sheet as an asset and stays there until the goods are sold. There is thus a delay in the recognition of cost as it affects the measurement of profit—as much as several months in some cases if the turnover of inventory is slow. This out-of-phase measurement of cost often results in a delayed recognition of the impact of inflation, a delay that destroys the value of the measurement.

The second element in this group is depreciation. This cost also originates on the balance sheet as an asset at the time of purchase of the equipment and then moves slowly over a period of time to the income statement, where it appears as an operating expense. Since inflation is driving up the replacement cost of such assets at the same time that management is writing them down—that is, reducing their book value—the charge for depreciation serves to undervalue the asset and to understate cost at the same time.

In short, the impact of inflation on the income statement is confined to the impact of the costs and expenses that flow from the balance sheet. All else is reasonably current and capable of direct measurement. Adjustment of the balance sheet values for the effect of inflation will thus resolve any needs for adjustment on the income statement itself.

The Valuation of Capital

Despite accounting rules to the contrary, the assumption that a borrower can write down a debt because it will be paid off in depreciated currency is not borne out by the history of inflation. The record, unfortunately, does not stand in favor of borrowers as long-term winners under any prolonged periods of inflation. Realistically then, the problem of the valuation of capital can be confined to the valuation of assets alone, values where the motivation is for survival rather than liquidation.

Under inflation, the assets of a business must be valued at expected replacement cost. Put simply, the value of the assets employed to produce the earnings should be expressed in the same currency as the earnings themselves. Both should be adjusted for inflation, and both should be stated in terms of current value. If the assets on the balance sheet are then also taken in order of appearance, the need for adjustment to *replacement value accounting* can be examined on a step-by-step basis.

The cash account is generally listed first and basically provides no problem in the measurement of current value. The dollar is worth less in terms of purchasing power, but the exact quantity is known and the impact all too measurable. Nothing, in short, is hidden from view in the valuation of this particular asset. Next in line is the measurement of accounts receivable, the balances due from customers in accordance with the terms of credit granted. Assuming that the collection of accounts is not past due to any great extent, inflation should cause no problem in the valuation of this asset either. If prices have been raised to offset higher costs, the increase is certainly measurable in the balance due, a balance that will shortly convert to cash in any event.

The problem in asset valuation will first surface with the inventory account, a tie-up of capital greater than either cash or receivables for most companies. The problem of valuation is compounded by the method of inventory accounting that the company elects to use. There are two basic methods—FIFO, or first-in-first-out, and LIFO, or last-in-first-out—along with various combinations of the two, such as average costing. The two basic methods do not deal with the physical movement of goods but with the movement and recognition of cost.

For example, the two methods might show the following comparison of results:

	FIFO	LIFO
Price	$1.00	$1.00
Cost	.50	1.25
Profit	$ .50	$ (.25)

Under FIFO accounting, the company will report a profit of 50 cents on every unit sold—and worse, will pay income tax on the reported profit—even though the latest recorded cost is $1.25 and a loss of 25 cents on every sale would be shown under LIFO accounting. The company is thus seriously overstating its profits, but with the lower first cost removed from the balance sheet, the remaining inventory is more nearly valued at the current cost of $1.25 per unit. With the use of LIFO, just the opposite occurs. Profits will not be inflated, but the inventory will be valued at the lower cost of 50 cents, resulting in a serious undervaluation of the asset.

Of the two, LIFO is clearly the preferable method under inflation, since it solves a major problem of inflated profits and an unnecessary cash drain in income taxes. It creates an unacceptable problem on the balance sheet, however, where undervalued assets can only lead to an underpricing of the product. If pricing is to be based on an objective rate of return on assets managed, then both sides of the equation must be corrected at the same time—both the statement of cost charged against income for the period and the valuation of the asset that served to produce the income.

A third method is thus required for the useful valuation of inventory under inflation. This method is called NIFO, or next-in-first-out accounting. It means that inventory will not be valued at the cost at which it was acquired or produced, but at what it is expected to cost next time around. At the same time, the charge for cost of goods sold on the income statement will reflect estimated replacement cost as well. Such a method may violate accounting principles, but it will definitely aid management in arriving at selling prices that are based on a replacement of values.

An even larger problem in asset valuation is found in the so-called fixed asset group of land, buildings, machinery, and the like. For many businesses, this will be the greatest concentration of asset investment and one where the use of capital is committed, not for weeks or months, but for years at a time. The greater tie-up of capital extending over a longer period of time creates a valuation problem by itself, but the problem is compounded by the method of depreciation that management elects to use in writing down the asset over its expected useful life. Applying the accelerated rates of depreciation allowable for tax purposes, for example, will simply hasten the process of undervaluation during periods of high inflation. Even with use of straight-line or normal depreciation rates, the spread between net book value and replacement cost will widen rapidly.

If, for example, an asset is purchased for $100,000 and given an estimated depreciable life of ten years at a straight-line rate of 10 percent a year, it would be fully written off by the end of the tenth year, down to a book value of zero. If the assumption is also made that the equipment will last exactly ten years in use and then have to be replaced with another unit capable of doing the same job, the company would find itself in the position shown in Figure 11. At an income tax rate of 50 percent, the company would have recovered one-half, or $50,000, of the investment through depreciation and taxes, an amount not necessarily present in cash, but evident in the accumulated net earnings. And while the company had been writing its $100,000 purchase down to $50,000 available to replace it, inflation had taken the replacement cost of a comparable piece of equipment to a new price level of $250,000, leaving the company $200,000 short of being able to replace the asset and stay in business.

If, at the same time, pricing for the product pro-

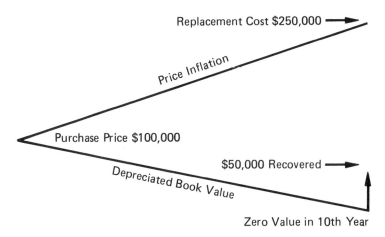

Figure 11.

duced by the equipment had been based on the declining value base of the asset, it is reasonable to suppose that prices had steadily been reduced over the same ten-year period. The impact on earnings is thus two-fold: prices have not been based on the replacement value of assets managed and therefore have not been high enough to provide for replacement of the assets under inflation. Even worse, since prices have been reduced in line with a declining base of asset value, the earnings have not even been sufficient to replace the assets at original cost.

Relief is needed in the form of indexation of asset values, indexation that will allow tax-deductible depreciation on replacement cost adjusted annually. To a great extent, this would conserve earnings for the replacement of productive assets instead of diverting those earnings to the tax collector as a hidden tax on capital. With or without the tax benefit, however, the fixed assets of a business must—like the value for inventory—be valued at replacement cost if the pricing base is to produce prices that, in turn, will eventually provide the means for replacement of the assets themselves.

This need raises the question of how to value a building, a piece of equipment, or a fleet of vehicles. Should they be valued at the current price of a brand new building or machine? And how is the replacement value to be computed on a piece of equipment when the original supplier has gone out of production on that particular model? The solutions to these and similar problems of bringing the net book value up to estimated replacement cost will not be found in the accounting rules for inflation. Financial Accounting Standards Board Rule 33 offers no more than a multiple-choice approach that does little but confuse the issue. The best approach will be found in the guideline issued by the Securities and Exchange Commission in 1976, when it first required reporting of replacement value in the 10-K reports of certain large companies. Apparently foreseeing the problems involved in different types of assets, it stated that the value should be the value of equivalent productive capacity, a standard that will serve well in moving the balance sheet from accounting fiction to economic reality.

Along with the question of what method to use in revaluing the fixed assets of the business, the question of where to get opinion on replacement value also requires direction. Management should itself be the best source of advice on the replacement cost of inventory under the recommended NIFO method for inflation, but it may have to seek outside help with respect to the replacement cost of land, buildings, and machinery. Two outside sources are generally available: experts in the field or indexes provided by an insurance agency for each category in the asset group. If neither of these are available, management should supply its own estimates, since even rough approximations will be preferable to no adjustment at all.

Finally, it would be best if the write-up of the fixed assets were brought on to the general ledger rather than held in memo accounts only. Since the change is apt to be a substantial one with substantial impact on pricing decisions, the increase in value employed should be recognized in the mainstream of measurement if it is to be regarded as a real rather than a statistical increase in capital. In doing so, it must be presented simply as an adjustment of values, not in any sense of measurement as a profit produced by the revaluation. A suggested entry on the books of account might, for example, read:

> Dr. Increase from Revaluation
> Cr. Surplus from Revaluation

The debit side of the entry will create a new asset account for the amount of the revaluation increment, while the credit will serve as a restatement of the value of the equity capital itself.

One further step is required on the income statement—that of recording an additional charge for depreciation on the revaluation increment for depreciable assets. Since this new layer of cost will not, at least for the present, be a tax-deductible charge, a separate account will be needed in the classification of operating expenses. At this point, with both the inventory and the fixed asset group valued at replacement cost, the balance sheet has been adjusted, for the time being, for the impact of inflation. The adjustments will have to be kept current in the future, with the frequency of review dependent on the rate of inflation itself. The income statement will now also reflect replacement cost, both in the cost of goods sold as well as in charges for depreciation. Both financial reports are thus again ready for use in the pricing process, but before the new prices can be determined, attention must be given to one other dimension that has also been changing with inflation.

The Adequacy of Profit

While inflation has been driving up the valuation base of the capital on which an objective rate of return will be placed to determine the prices required, inflation has also been pushing up the required rate of return on capital itself. One inevitable consequence of inflation is found in a major increase in interest rates— one step in a cycle where inflation creates a growing shortage of capital, combining with actions taken by government to curb the supply of credit, and all leading to a higher cost for money.

The increase is first noted in the *prime rate,* the rate charged by banks to their most credit-worthy customers. The prime rate for money sets in motion the interest rates for government securities, savings accounts, corporate bonds, and finally to the economic rate of return required at the level of average industrial risk. This risk/return relationship is shown in Figure 12, a relationship that may serve to explain more fully the earlier statement that the cost of capital for the non-regulated business will equal approximately one and two-thirds times the average prime rate.

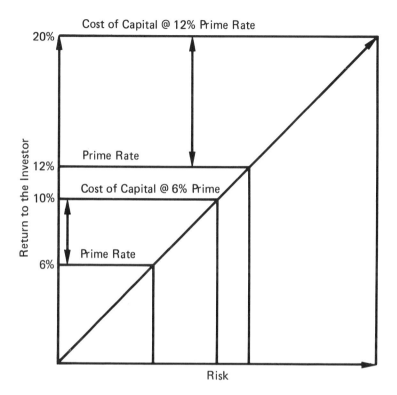

Figure 12. Risk/return relationship.

Prior to inflation, with a prime rate holding steady at a level of 6 percent, the cost of capital for business averaged 10 percent after taxes, a measurement of the return required by the investor as compensation for risk. As the prime rate increases with inflation, so does the cost of capital, the two moving in tandem to levels of higher and higher relative risk. In the example shown, an average prime rate of 12 percent will thus translate into a 20 percent cost of capital rate for business, a spread dictated both by logic and by the behavior of price/earnings ratios in relation to interest rates. Projections of the cost of capital, however, must be based on average expectations of the future, not a record of the past.

Final Steps

With steps taken to deal with all three problem areas imposed on business measurements by inflation, the way is now clear to repeat the steps of the pricing process and to determine the new price level required. The measurement of cost has been corrected, the valuation of capital adjusted, and the adequacy of profits put into proper perspective. The only barrier remaining may be the marketplace itself. The natural inclination to simply pass the cost of inflation along to the customer in higher and higher prices may soon meet a point of resistance where other solutions will be needed. A proper management of pricing will take steps to explore those other solutions first, making sure that proposed increases in price are not built on a foundation of waste and inefficiency. Taken in order of priority, these steps include:

1. *A review of capital required.* This should be done in terms of the *need* for each of the assets supplied by the capital, a need that can best be defined in terms of normal or average turnover rates related to the planned volume of sales. The review should start with this step if for no other reason than because the management of capital is often the most neglected part of the structure. If unnecessary levels of investment are built in, it is obvious that prices developed from such a base will be unnecessarily high.

2. *A review of period expense support.* This review must challenge all levels of supporting period expense built into the pricing base, accepting each only on the basis of need, not on the record of historical use. Like excess capital, excess costs will only serve to produce unacceptable prices.

3. *A review of product design.* This step is placed third in order of priority since the basic design of the product and its resulting direct variable cost of production are normally under continuing review in most operations. Inflation, however, will force a new look at all elements of cost, and this area is not exempt from change.

4. *A review of capacity utilization.* This final step calls for an analysis of the basis for measuring capacity, to ensure that optimum capacity includes the optimum use of capital and that the utilization of capacity is also planned at an optimum point that will encompass both the efficiency of operations and the efficiency of capital employed.

Once these steps have been accomplished, then, and only then, should prices be increased to meet the demands of inflation. If the higher prices are based on efficiency rather than waste, they will represent a need that will receive recognition in the marketplace. In the so-called perfect market, prices will adjust to a level that allows for the recovery of all necessary costs. And while perfect markets seldom exist, the probability under inflation is that prices will tend to move in this direction rather than away from it. In essence, for all its evils, inflation may force business to a more efficient approach to pricing than might have been possible at a more leisurely pace of events.

9

Adapting
Pricing Strategies
to Business Cycles

If all business moved on a straight and level path, planning and controlling would be greatly simplified. Without the peaks and valleys of prosperity and depression, without the changing demands of war and peace, and particularly without the impact of inflation or deflation on business measurements and decisions, the path ahead would be quite predictable. Sales volume would respond to anticipated market growth, costs would increase in proportion to size, and profit requirements would remain at a constant rate of return on capital consistent with an unchanging prime rate for funds.

Productive capacity could be matched exactly with demand, and an optimum level of utilization maintained on a planned schedule of output for an indefinite period of time. Pricing could thus be reduced to the routine task of simply matching a constant need against a constant market—a pricing strategy that would contemplate no need for change.

The reality is obviously a bit more complex—a business environment where the only constant factor is change itself. Every business will experience good years and bad years, with reports of record profits followed by operations at or below the breakeven point. And when such changes inevitably occur, management is forced to adapt to the changing demands of the marketplace, to changing levels of pricing requirements, and to changing attitudes of pricing acceptance. In this process, most managements are simply reacting to the apparent needs of the moment, making a series of tactical changes completely without strategic purpose or direction.

If, for example, a NIFO, or next-in-first-out, method of inventory accounting had been adopted under conditions of spiraling costs during a period of inflation, a strategic plan would dictate that the same logic also had validity during subsequent periods of deflation. Such a method would continue to support the concept of pricing on the basis of replacement cost, with consistent reasoning in either direction.

The need for such a pricing strategy exists, but the planning required to understand the need usually does not—not unless management can somehow learn to anticipate such changes and to develop a method of predicting not only that changes will occur, but predicting also both the timing and the direction those changes will take. Such a method exists in the study of cycles, the study of the regularity with which certain events are found to recur, a regularity that in many cases implies the predictability of such changes on a scheduled basis over equal periods of time.

One of the more familiar cycles in business is the *product life cycle* on the well-known bell-shaped curve shown in Figure 13. Every product will go through this cycle from the alpha of inception to the omega of obsolescence. The journey is predictable and certain—the only unknown being the length of time between the two points. The regularity of the cycle behavior then lies in the fact that when Product A reaches its point of obsolescence, the cycle for Product B, which replaces it, will conform to the same pattern, a pattern

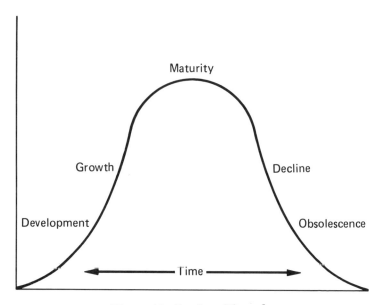

Figure 13. Product life cycle.

that will inevitably be followed by Product C and all subsequent new or improved products in the future. Knowing that this cycle will take place for every product suggests a strategic approach to pricing that will follow the same path, a path that recognizes the changing limitations, opportunities, and eventual restrictions of the marketplace.

Development

The early stages of product development and design will entail engineering and start-up costs that normally cannot be recovered in pricing the initial volume of sales. Pricing for an objective rate of return on capital employed during this phase will thus call for a strategy of *forward pricing,* one based on projected levels of volume, cost, and investment. Assuming that some market research has preceded the development of the product, estimates of market demand, method of distribution, and targeted price levels are expected to be available along with the estimated cost of production, period expense support, and capital investment requirements.

The strategic plan at this point should thus be based on capturing a future share of market over a period of time at a targeted level of profitability. Inherent in this strategy will be an evaluation of the value-added content of the product, a determination of the probable price/cost sensitivity or volume sensitivity in the marketplace.

A choice must also be made about the price level to be used to introduce the new product. A pricing strategy will call either for a high initial price to be followed

by price reductions as demand builds up, or for a lower
price as a plan to discourage early competition. Either
way, pricing would be planned in relation to the product life cycle, not taken in a series of trial-and-error
steps in an after-the-fact reaction to competitive pressures.

Growth and Maturity

The growth phase of the life cycle will cover the
period of investment and expansion required to meet
an increased demand for the product. It will also be a
period of increasing competition, as more companies
enter the market with a profusion of terms, discounts,
and price adjustments. The tendency will be to sacrifice
immediate profit for market share, and substantial
overcapacity may be created as all competitors strive
for the same goal. The pricing strategy that will best
survive this shakeout will be one that looks beyond the
short-term attainment of volume in favor of a longer
term plan for profitability.

Planning, rather than reacting, will involve a careful management of capital, an optimum utilization of
capacity, and a consistent application of the pricing
curve as a strategic management tool. When market
growth reaches a leveling off point, indicating the maturity phase of the life cycle, investment in productive
capacity should be held to the level of replacement and
working capital commitments maintained at ongoing
levels rather than increased in expectation of further
growth. And while the duration of the maturity phase
may prove difficult to predict, a pricing strategy that

underestimates this phase may prove more profitable than continuing attempts to extend it.

Decline and Obsolescence

Every product will eventually reach the end point of complete obsolescence, a point where it will be replaced with a newer design, an improved model, or a new and totally different method or invention. The changeover is simply a matter of degree, either culminating in a period of gradual transition or ending abruptly, with greater impact.

The pricing strategy during this final phase of the life cycle should be based on an orderly plan of withdrawal from the market, a strategy that starts with a gradual liquidation of investment. This is the time to stop investing in even the replacement of productive capacity and to end all commitments to product improvement or redesign. Pricing based on such a plan can be reduced as necessary in contemplation of lower asset investment and diminishing needs for period expense support. A strategy to eventually capture 100 percent of a declining market through scheduled price reductions may reduce current levels of income, but by maximizing cash flow during this terminal phase, it actually achieves the lowest cost of obsolescence and hence the highest final profitability.

Business Cycles

While the several stages of the product life cycle may appear obvious and susceptible to predictable periods

of pricing needs, what is not so obvious in business is
the fact that cycles of an entirely different nature will
also occur, taking place within the span of the life cycle
itself. A study of such cycles has found that they occur
at predictable intervals, no matter what technology or
new inventions are developed, no matter what the pol-
itics or the economics of the period. Cycles will occur
in business when any purchase that can be deferred *is*
deferred, and knowledge of this behavior pattern can
greatly assist management in judging the timing for the
introduction of new products, for increasing or curtail-
ing production, and for carrying out a strategic plan
for pricing. The technique is as follows.

The figures for monthly orders or shipments are
listed for several years back and then accumulated into
a 12-month moving total, dropping the figure for the
month in the prior year as each new month is added.
The history of the first year is thus locked into the first
moving total 12 months later, so that a ten-year record
by month would be needed to provide a nine-year trend
of moving totals. Each moving total is then divided by
the level of a year ago to produce a percentage measurement of the *rate of change,* an index referred to as
the 12/12 pressure, indicating the cyclical behavior of
the business. Table 26 shows the accumulated data for
Company A, starting with the dollar value of orders
received in January 1973.

The 12/12 rate of change starts at the end of the
second year, yielding eight years of cyclical behavior
out of a ten-year record of monthly orders received.
The 12-month moving total as of December 1974 is
measured as only 81.5 percent of the total for December 1973, establishing a rate of change that can then
be used to describe the pattern of the business cycle.

Year	Month	Monthly Orders	12-Month Moving Total	12/12%
1973	Jan	1,720		
	Feb	1,755		
	March	2,069		
	April	1,789		
	May	1,658		
	June	2,078		
	July	1,936		
	Aug	2,134		
	Sep	2,425		
	Oct	2,355		
	Nov	2,063		
	Dec	1,629	23,611	
1974	Jan	1,642	23,533	
	Feb	1,836	23,614	
	March	1,831	23,376	
	April	1,789	23,376	
	May	1,756	23,474	
	June	1,666	23,062	
	July	1,636	22,762	
	Aug	1,642	22,270	
	Sep	1,417	21,262	
	Oct	1,658	20,565	
	Nov	1,335	19,837	
	Dec	1,045	19,253	81.5%
1975	Jan	1,600	19,211	81.6%
	Feb	1,257	18,632	78.9%
	March	1,392	18,193	77.8%
	April	1,566	17,970	76.9%
	May	1,587	17,801	75.8%
	June	1,664	17,799	77.2%
	July	1,574	17,737	77.9%
	Aug	1,737	17,832	80.1%
	Sep	1,934	18,349	86.3%
	Oct	2,309	19,000	92.4%
	Nov	1,936	19,601	98.8%
	Dec	1,654	20,210	105.0%

Note, for example, that the 12/12 pressure starting in February 1975 marked the beginning of a down cycle to a low of 75.8 percent in May *in spite of the fact that the monthly level of orders received was actually increasing during the same period.* Figures for the following years were then added, and the 12/12 rate of change was plotted as a *cycle curve,* as shown in Figure 14. A defi-

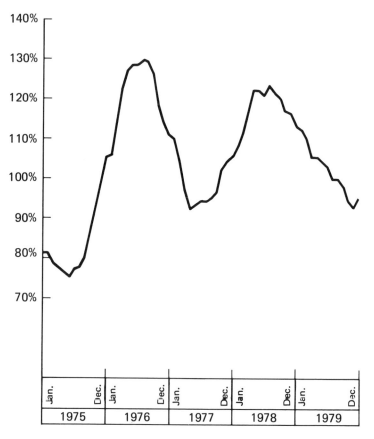

Figure 14. Cycle curve.

nite cycle of orders received began to emerge that suggested substantial implications in planning if a repetition of the cycle could be expected in the future. Not the least of the implications was the possibility of a strategy for pricing in anticipation of the cycle change.

This study was initially made at the end of 1979 and continued into 1980, when production backlogs were found to have had a delaying effect on the expected upturn in monthly orders. The upturn came, however, at the end of that year, as shown in Figure 15, and management began to have confidence in the predictability evidenced by this new technique. Prices were cautiously increased in expectation of an upward cycle for 1981, an expectation fully justified by subsequent events.

As the year progressed, the actual trend was plotted as a solid line on the curve, and while the final results did not drop the cycle as low as anticipated, they moved in the direction predicted and in the same order of magnitude. More importantly, the 12/12 cycle had proved its worth as a strategic tool for budgeting and for planning the pricing action required.

A peak in the up cycle has since been projected for mid-1982, and operating budgets and pricing actions planned accordingly. As one company manager put it, "The key point is: With cycle forecasting you have already been prepared for the decline; for perhaps six months you have seen it coming."

In another company, Company B, an opposite situation existed. The top of an up cycle had apparently been reached in the latter half of 1980, and a downturn appeared imminent for 1981. Assuming that the coming down cycle might equal the previous low on the curve experienced about three years earlier, a curve

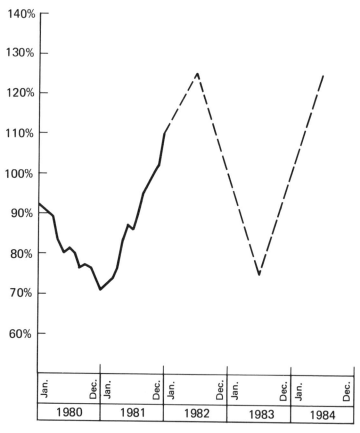

Figure 15.

was first drawn for 1981 from a peak index of 170 percent to a low of 105 percent—a curve matching the top
and the bottom of the previous cycle. The calculations
were then reversed.

Working backward from the assumed 12/12 pressure curve, the 12-month moving totals were first established as though the changes had already taken

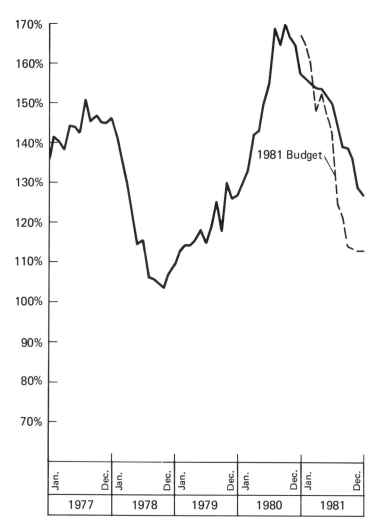

Figure 16.

place. Next the moving totals themselves were backed off to determine the amount of each month's sales. The monthly sales figures arrived at by this method were then adjusted for seasonal variations and other known factors, and the final budget was reentered as the dotted line on the cycle curve shown in Figure 16.

Based on the trend thus indicated for the year, the budgets for supporting cost and investment were planned accordingly. These budgets then formed the base for a pricing strategy for the coming year—a strategy to avoid price increases that might otherwise be made in response to inflation by a program of greater efficiency in the use of capital, coupled with a planned reduction in the level of period expense support.

In summary, pricing cannot be considered as a static situation where business trends are seen as moving in only a single direction over an extended period of time. Forces exist that cause trends to move in two directions simultaneously—upward on one cycle over the life of the product and both upward and downward in periodic cycles during the course of the life cycle itself. Successful pricing for profit is thus dependent on two fundamental measurements—*need,* based on an objective rate of return on capital, and *opportunity,* based on the study and interpretation of business cycles.

Index